PRAISE FOR *THE G......*

'An engrossing, illuminating and often disquieting study of
Scott Morrison. Sean Kelly's forensic analysis of the man he describes
as the "symbolic perfection of a certain version of Australia" compels
us all to consider our complicity in his creation.'
NIKI SAVVA

'It's been almost impossible to get a handle on Scott Morrison.
Until now. Sean Kelly has done it, comprehensively.'
BARRIE CASSIDY

'I used to think that ScoMo was just a daggy dad who loves making
curries and paying off his mortgage. But after reading this insightful,
funny and absolutely maddening dissection of the man, I can now
clearly see him for what he is. Sean Kelly exposes Morrison with wit
and righteous precision. Go Sharks!' **TOM BALLARD**

'One of the best things I've read in a long time'
NICK FEIK, EDITOR, *THE MONTHLY*

'Excellent' **ANNABEL CRABB**

'The political book of the year' **CAROLINE OVERINGTON**

'Brilliantly analytical, thoughtful and intensely researched'
SALLY RUGG

'Sean Kelly's *The Game: A Portrait of Scott Morrison* is a tour de force, the
most perceptive and complex account we yet have of our current prime
minister ... Subtle, probing intelligence and lucid, readable prose.'
JUDITH BRETT

'A very good book. Captures the emptiness, the black hole that is
Scott Morrison.' **MIKE CARLTON**

'Outstanding. The subtlety of the psychological insights and the steady hand, the weighing and testing of evidence, slowly reveal Morrison for what he truly is.' MARK McKENNA

'Not only is Sean Kelly the most elegant of the next generation of Australian political writers, he understands that Australians *chose* Scott Morrison in 2019. It wasn't a miracle. It said – and continues to say – something about us ... This is a tremendous, subtle, dispassionate analysis of a unique prime minister, our first leader for whom the dark and considerable arts of marketing lie at the very heart of the political endeavour.' HUGH RIMINTON

'*The Game* is a brilliant deconstruction of Scott Morrison's place in Australian politics. The prose of Sean Kelly is an antidote to the ScoMo persona: such great weight, and never blustering for the sake of it.' LECH BLAINE

'This is a cracker of a book. A thoughtful, fascinating, devastating examination of Morrison's personality, the way he plays politics, and the political game itself. Also enlightening on us, the voters.' LAURIE OAKES

'A terrific book. Sean Kelly ... brings an original, forensic take to his analysis. Many politics books look at strategy, this looks deeply at personality too.' LEIGH SALES

'This book is a beauty – and Morrison has indeed acted in recent days just as you'd expect on the basis of Sean [Kelly]'s analysis of his leadership and character.' FRANK BONGIORNO

'Sean Kelly writes elegantly and clearly. He understands how government and politics works. Delivers a keen eye for detail and perceptions as sharp as you'll find outside of an Attica kitchen.' DENNIS ATKINS

'Never thought I would honestly find myself thinking "I can't wait to read a book about Scott Morrison" but Sean Kelly is that good.'
ALEX LEE

'Got my hands on an early copy of this and it's good. According to Niki Savva it's "engrossing, illuminating". Very strong analysis.'
SAMANTHA MAIDEN

'This is a terrific dive into the construct that is ScoMo – feels at times more like a literary critique – in a good way!'
PETER LEWIS, DIRECTOR CENTRE FOR RESPONSIBLE TECHNOLOGY

THE GAME

THE GAME

A PORTRAIT OF SCOTT MORRISON

SEAN KELLY

Published by Black Inc.,
an imprint of Schwartz Books Pty Ltd
Level 1, 221 Drummond Street
Carlton VIC 3053, Australia
enquiries@blackincbooks.com
www.blackincbooks.com

9781760643119 (paperback)
9781743821985 (ebook)

A catalogue record for this
book is available from the
National Library of Australia

Cover image: Lukas Coch / AAP Images
Cover and text design by Tristan Main
Typesetting by Typography Studio

Printed in Australia by McPherson's Printing Group

MIX
Paper from
responsible sources
FSC
www.fsc.org   FSC® C001695

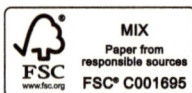

To Anne-Louise and Arlo

Dearer to us the falsehood that exalts
Than hosts of baser truths.

PUSHKIN, AS QUOTED BY CHEKHOV

Austrians can only tolerate seriousness as a joke.

THOMAS BERNHARD

A MAN

APPEARANCES

In 2015, the first episode of the fifth season of *Kitchen Cabinet* screened. The format of the popular television show was straightforward: the host, Annabel Crabb, would arrive, smiling, at the home of a politician. The politician would cook a meal; in exchange, Crabb would provide dessert. During the cooking, and then over the meal, the two would chat.

Crabb occupied a unique place in the Australian political landscape. She was an insightful analyst, but rather than adopting the dour or sententious attitude struck by most political experts, she was charming, friendly, witty. Instead of unfashionable suits, she wore brightly coloured dresses. She had made a name for herself in newspapers, with arch and elegant prose, then had successfully made the shift to television, becoming one of the biggest stars at the national broadcaster. A promotional kit distributed to the press that year featured a photo of Crabb dressed in yellow period costume as Marie Antoinette, smiling quizzically over her shoulder at the camera; in one hand she was holding a small slice of cake. (The publicists evidently judged this too subtle: with her other hand she held a newspaper with the headline 'Let Them Eat Cake!'.)

That year's season was met with uncommon rage. Columns

denouncing the show began to appear in the press. Crabb was forced to defend the program in interviews and in a column of her own. Even before the show screened, there was the scent of controversy in the air. Crabb told *The Guardian*: 'I've already had some feedback on social media from people saying, "Oh, I won't watch. How could you even speak to that evil man?", which I think is beyond ridiculous. What is the point of refusing to even countenance someone who is now so influential over all our lives?'

That 'evil man' was Scott Morrison, a senior minister in the Liberal government. His frame was large, giving the impression that, at some point in the past, he may have been well-built. His facial features were large too; he looked a little like a friendly ogre. His hair had receded quite a bit. What remained was tufty, mostly grey and white, in the final stages of retreat from the brown it had once been. For the more casual setting of *Kitchen Cabinet*, he was dressed, predictably enough for a middle-aged conservative politician, in a polo shirt, though possibly he had not bought it for himself: the colour was somewhere between mauve and wisteria. He was forty-seven and looked cheerily indestructible.

Morrison's appearance on the show had been heavily promoted. The press kit read, 'Morrison is at ease in the kitchen as he prepares a Sri Lankan fish curry, chapatis and samosas, or – as his staff hilariously call them – "ScoMosas".' The kit also reported that after accepting the role of immigration minister – the job he had held before moving to social services – Morrison had 'succeeded in his brief of stopping the asylum-seeker boats'.

The television producers no doubt hoped his appearance on the show would divide and provoke viewers, which it did, though perhaps not in the way they had expected. Attacks coalesced around the idea that Crabb was allowing politicians, Morrison in particular, a chance to seduce her viewers through the easy format of a soft lifestyle show, rather than interrogating them about their policies. In the first and sharpest critique, Amy McQuire argued journalism was 'not about humanising those in power, it's about humanising those who are let down by those in power.'

Defending herself against the outrage, Crabb mentioned one argument she had found more persuasive than most, from TV critic Ben Pobjie, who wrote: 'What a government minister is like at home – or in the kitchen – is irrelevant to the country: what matters is what they do. And the more we get to know them personally the more we fall for the lie that "what they're really like" is important.' Crabb's response was this:

> I don't think you can possibly separate what people are like from what they do. Political leaders – like every single one of us – are shaped by the things that have happened to them and to the people close to them. Those factors – what they're like – exert a considerable and usually invisible influence over the most important decisions a political leader will ever make. Namely: which issues they are going to choose to die in a ditch for, which they will pop in the too-hard basket, which they might compromise on. This is the stuff that realistically drives the political process. And fleshy, human, and deeply subjective stuff it is too. Knowing what a person is like is powerful. Why should it only be political journalists and insiders who get to see it?

Much of the rage could be traced to a single notorious incident, from Morrison's time in Opposition. In 2010, towards the end of the year, when most politicians were already on holiday, fifty asylum seekers died in a wreck. Their wooden boat crashed into rocks, and was then smashed by the ocean into the cliffs of Christmas Island. At that point, it came apart. This was in the early morning. One local told the ABC that he woke to a 'sort of synchronised screaming'. Another said, 'Ladies and men, babies as well, young kids … they were screaming, screaming for help.' Three days later, the authorities called off their search and rescue efforts.

Since 2001, Christmas Island – 1550 kilometres to the north-west of the Australian mainland – had been used to hold asylum seekers. Because it was a shorter trip from Indonesia than mainland Australia was, it had also become a destination for people wishing to claim asylum in Australia. The survivors of the wreck were detained on the island but asked that their dead family members be buried on the mainland. The Labor government agreed. Nine weeks later, near the end of summer, several were flown to Sydney, along with other relatives of the dead, to attend the funerals.

A report later that week in *The Canberra Times* recounted an extraordinary political attack:

Opposition immigration spokesman Scott Morrison told 2GB radio he believed Australians would be 'angry' to learn the Government was paying for grieving families to fly from Christmas Island to the mainland to attend the funerals.

'Well, there's nothing in the refugee convention which covers this situation and places an obligation on us and I think people would be, rightly from what they've heard, angry about this,' Morrison said. 'I think they'll be wanting an explanation from the minister.' And they did: talkback radio switchboards, from 2GB to Canberra's 666 ABC, lit up with irate callers. Morrison repeated his criticism of the Government paying for the funerals throughout the day of the funeral.

That night television bulletins carried heart-rending scenes of a woman screaming and collapsing in grief, and a bereft little boy now identified as nine-year-old Seena Akhlaqi Sheikhdost, who lost both parents and a brother in the tragedy, clinging to relatives for comfort.

By Wednesday it was Morrison who was forced to issue an apology for his words, saying the timing of them was 'insensitive'.

Morrison had not apologised – at no point did he utter the word 'sorry'. He would have known this was unnecessary. An expression of regret in public life, however carefully worded, acts like a gas: however contained at first, it quickly spreads; however specific, however finely put, it is taken as a broad apology for whatever sin has been committed.

Here is what Morrison told the right-wing radio host Ray Hadley on Sydney radio station 2GB:

HADLEY: You want to clear up some confusion apparently, my staff tell me?

MORRISON: Well, look, Ray, I think you summarised it well. No one is ever going to accuse me, I think, of not taking this matter up to the government and holding them to account but timing in terms of comments, I think, is very important and the timing of my comments over the last twenty-four hours was insensitive and was inappropriate. I know probably more than anyone how strongly people feel about this issue, how angry they get about the costs that are involved and I share that anger and I want to see that changed but there is a time and a place. I rarely leave things on the field when it comes to this issue, Ray, as you know, but if you step over the mark I think you have got to say so and I am prepared to do that, but the government shouldn't take that as a leave pass.

After some more discussion, Hadley sought to wrap things up:

HADLEY: Okay, so you resile from what you, you back away from what you said yesterday . . .

MORRISON: I back away from the timing of it, Ray.

HADLEY: The timing of it, okay.

MORRISON: That was insensitive and it was inappropriate and I am happy to cop to that.

As some observers pointed out at the time, Morrison's expression of regret was strikingly narrow. Rather than putting what had happened behind him, he repeated his complaint, in emotive terms: voters were angry and so was he. He called for things to change and warned the Labor government the matter was not over. Only his timing was insensitive. When Hadley attempted to broaden the apology to include the words themselves, Morrison immediately corrected him, repeating his point: he backed away only from the timing.

The other remarkable thing about the passage is how much of it Morrison spends reviewing his own performance and giving it high marks. Morrison told listeners that 'no one is ever going to accuse me of not taking this matter up to the government' because 'I rarely leave things on the field when it comes to this issue', and 'I know probably more than anyone how . . . angry they get about the costs that are involved and I share that anger'. In a discussion of funerals following a shipwreck in which fifty people had died, Morrison seemed mostly concerned with bolstering his image and addressing a fear that his conservative supporters might take his regret as a sign that he was going soft.

There was another odd moment halfway through the interview. Hadley raised the costs of hotel accommodation for other asylum seekers. Morrison agreed with Hadley, saying:

> I think that is right and the story that appeared in yesterday's *Telegraph* was as a result of our digging into Senate Estimates to reveal these costs, and these costs are big, they are great, they are getting bigger. They are not going to go away, they are going to keep increasing and I have to show a little more compassion than I did yesterday, I am happy to admit that.

Morrison's attack on costs comes with the rhythm of a preacher building to a crescendo. The final words, about compassion, come out of nowhere. They are a non sequitur. It is as though Morrison suddenly realised he had allowed his rising anger at these rising costs – 'they are big, they are great, they are getting bigger' – to get away from him, and that he was doing this interview for quite another reason, to which he then mechanically returned. It was an odd, robotic response, as though a safety switch had kicked in before the actual rush of feeling became too much. Something real had been glimpsed and had to be locked away.

The precise words that Morrison used in this swerve back to his intended topic were interesting too. He did not say that he needed to be more compassionate; he said that he had realised he needed to *show* a little more compassion. In its apparent concern only with impressions, this matched the very deliberately restricted regret Morrison had chosen to express, avoiding substance altogether.

Morrison was sharply attacked. Former Liberal prime minister Malcolm Fraser said it was politics 'at its basest'. Another former leader of Morrison's party, John Hewson, said the comments were 'insensitive, lacking appropriate compassion, even inhumane'. Journalist Peter Hartcher wrote that Morrison was 'the greatest grub in the federal parliament'.

———

Two years later, a long profile of Morrison was published in *Good Weekend* magazine, distributed with *The Sydney Morning Herald* and *The Age*. The journalist, Jane Cadzow, began with a story about

Morrison's appointment to the immigration portfolio, evidently heard firsthand:

> Scott Morrison was in the car when the call came. It was December 2009 and Tony Abbott, the new federal Opposition leader, was offering him a position in his shadow ministry. Morrison's wife, Jenny, who was driving, listened to his end of the conversation. Then she said, 'Anything, as long as it's not immigration. Tell me it's not immigration.' Morrison looked at her. 'It's immigration,' he said.
>
> He smiles about that now.

Cadzow's piece is a fine example of the magazine profiler's art – and of the power of a writer over their subject. It is written in sufficiently detached a tone not to repel readers, who are always on the lookout, whether they know it or not, for writers too obviously biased. But this is a strategy, not an indication of actual detachment, because it is clear Cadzow does not like Morrison, or at least does not find herself able to morally approve of his approach to refugees.

Cadzow was in a bind. Profiles like this are commissioned when a politician is on the rise; major newspapers expect their journalists not to take sides. Editors are always alert to the possibility they will receive angry phone calls from politicians. They are happy to defend their journalists but want to make sure there is something to defend, which comes down to a question of whether they can reasonably respond that the reporting was 'fair'. After all, who can say where a rising politician might end up?

Cadzow gives her editors what they need: there is plenty of praise for Morrison quoted in the article, and her own opinion is never openly put. She employs two techniques to make her case against him. The first lies in the structure she has chosen. At one point, Cadzow quotes a senior Liberal: 'I think there are different parts to Scott. One is a genuine, nice guy, a good family man with good instincts. And then there's another part, which is pure ambition.' Though Cadzow does not make it explicit, this is the structuring principle of the piece. A paragraph or two on Morrison's personal life, including his religion, is followed by a paragraph or two on his hostility to refugees. We are, in effect, being asked whether these 'different parts to Scott' are compatible: is it possible to be a good family man of religious faith and to treat refugees the way that he has treated them?

Her other technique is simple enough: she allows Morrison to hang himself. Her profile is full of damning details, like that smile for the story about being given the immigration portfolio. In her final paragraph, a miniature masterpiece, Cadzow deploys both techniques at once: her themes of cruelty and religious hypocrisy meet in Morrison's honest answer to a straightforward question:

One afternoon, I ask Morrison if he prays for asylum seekers. 'Of course I do,' he says. 'I think that's part of any Christian's practice.' A pause. 'I'm not saying I do it every day. I'm not saying I do it every month.' But occasionally, yes, he includes them in his prayers.

Halfway through the episode of *Kitchen Cabinet*, shot at the South Coast house where Morrison holidays with his family, Crabb and Morrison are sitting outside. Soon, the sun will set and the sky will turn a brilliant pink as they eat the cake that Crabb has prepared, but right now the curry Morrison has cooked is laid out before them and the sky is blue. Crabb asks about the moment Morrison found out he had the immigration portfolio – perhaps she had read about it in the Cadzow piece. Morrison enjoys telling the story.

'This was back in 2009, and Tony had just become leader. We were driving to my parents' place to pick up the kids, I think. It was that Sunday afternoon, I think, when those calls are made, and I saw Tony Abbott's name come up. Jenny was driving, and I was in the passenger seat. And she just looked at me and said, "Anything but immigration. Anything but immigration."'

Morrison mimes holding the phone up to his mouth. '"Oh, righto, mate. Yes, yep, of course."' He mimes putting the phone down. '"Immigration."'

At this point in his telling of the story, he giggles. 'And we managed to stay on the road.' He giggles again. 'She understood. While Jen is not political, she's not naive to what politics is about.'

The form of the story is familiar, like an old joke: saying out loud that you don't want something and then immediately being given that exact thing. And it is clear, from the similarity of the story to the Cadzow version, that for Morrison it is an old story that has, with time, hardened into its final form. It is easy to watch this exchange and not think anything of it. If you consider it for just a moment, though, you realise the elements don't match. Here is a government minister, sitting in a pleasant rented holiday house on the South

Coast, recounting the story of how he came to be a famously hard-line immigration minister in the form of an amusing family anecdote, the type trotted out at Christmas lunch. A year after the events in the story take place, he will use his position to question the wisdom of spending public money to enable a little boy to attend the funerals of his parents. In the camps for which he had responsibility, one man was murdered during a riot. Another died from a treatable illness because he was not flown to an Australian hospital in time. When allegations that children had been sexually abused in those camps became public, Morrison diverted attention from them by making unfounded accusations against those whom the government suspected had leaked the allegations to media. All of this occurred in the years before he told this story on *Kitchen Cabinet*.

In a few moments, Morrison has enacted the dilemma at the heart of Cadzow's article: the apparently easy coexistence of a decent family man and a politician able to cause pain to people already suffering terribly.

Political hypocrisy is hardly uncommon, but this is something of another order. Morrison's behaviour is downright strange. He giggles as he talks, still tickled by the event, even after all these retellings. It would not be out of place in a film directed by David Lynch, displaying what the novelist David Foster Wallace described as 'a particular kind of irony where the very macabre and the very mundane combine in such a way as to reveal the former's containment within the latter'.

There is another element of the episode that is perhaps even stranger. A few years before, a long civil war had ended in Sri Lanka. After the war, Tamils faced retribution: many were abducted by men in white vans and tortured. Some fled the country in fear. In 2013, while in Opposition, Morrison travelled to Sri Lanka. There, he met with the government – the same government feared by the Tamils. He promised to help supply the Sri Lankan navy with boats to help stop asylum seekers leaving Sri Lanka. Then, as Australia's immigration minister, he was responsible for handing fleeing Tamils back to the Sri Lankan government.

Morrison could have chosen, as the meal he would cook for Crabb, anything in the world. He chose a Sri Lankan curry, and he had been inspired, he said, by that 2013 trip to Sri Lanka.

If we find ourselves wondering how to make sense of these apparent oddities, Morrison offers us two clues. The first comes when Crabb asks him about his manner at the time:

CRABB: Your role in that operation required you to be a certain way, didn't it? You had to have a certain demeanour in your press conferences. You became very well known for your militaristic, impassive press conferences. Was that part of the strategy?

MORRISON: Well, it was deliberate. It started well before the election, before we came to government – because those who are thinking of making the voyage, and more importantly those who are thinking of running the smuggling, needed to understand that if we were elected, their worst nightmare had arrived.

Later, he says:

I do get a lot of people ascribing motives and positions to me, and I just see that as their issue, not mine. What should I have done? Not stop the boats? What should I have done? I'm pleased that in the things the prime minister has asked me to do, I've had some success . . . Look, he asked me to do something, I'll do it as best as I can. If that means people go, 'He gets some things done, isn't that good', well, good – what's the alternative?

In the first instance, he suggests that his demeanour was a front, taken on for strategic purposes: a necessary performance. He had said that the year before, as well: 'As [a] minister or in Opposition, people would take their cue from my demeanour and posture and they needed to know it was going to be hard as a rock.' In the second, he makes clear that he was merely doing a job the prime minister had asked him to do.

Morrison is, at the same time, claiming his achievement and distancing himself from it. He stopped the boats and is happy to use the phrase – but he did not choose to stop the boats, he was doing what he was told. And the man you saw doing that, night after night on your television? He was only a concoction.

This is the brilliance of the recurring story about Jenny's dismay at Morrison receiving the immigration portfolio. It is like one of those cartoons where a little angel sits on one shoulder, a little devil on the other. In Morrison's story, Abbott is the devil, asking him to do what he must to achieve his ambitions, while Jenny is the angel, voicing the objections of his conscience. A cartoon character has to choose between the two – but Morrison does not. The purpose of

Jenny in this story is to make clear that Morrison has a conscience; the purpose of Abbott is to make clear that he will do his duty, whatever the moral consequences. The two find resolution in the proposition that, in accepting Abbott's offer and successfully carrying out his instructions – a success that would help Morrison, within a few years, become prime minister – he was only playing a role.

———

The story of Morrison finding out he had the immigration portfolio has had at least one other outing. This time it is Jenny telling the story, and the tale assumes its appropriate tone: 'I said, when he got off the phone, "Just tell me it's not Immigration", and he said, "It's Immigration". That was incredibly hard.'

In each version, there is a surprising omission. We never learn what Morrison himself thought about the appointment. We can guess, though, from the openness with which Jenny's difficulty has been described to us. There is a good chance Morrison was pleased. It was a promotion to a high-profile portfolio. Morrison was making his way.

There have been suggestions that when Morrison was later moved from the portfolio into social services he was not happy with the change. Soon, he must have recognised the gift he had been given. For years he had played the part of tough immigration spokesman. Now he had the chance to leave that role behind, to create a new, softer image, and to demonstrate to voters that their impression of him had been a limited one, perhaps even incorrect.

The story told from Jenny's perspective comes from a long profile of Morrison which appeared in that oddly named monthly magazine *The Australian Women's Weekly* in August 2015, not very long before the *Kitchen Cabinet* episode. A friendly photo shoot in the *Women's Weekly* is a time-honoured ritual for prime ministerial aspirants, a way both to reach readers who are not necessarily deeply engaged by politics and to signal to those who are that your ambition is strong and getting stronger. The piece ended like this: 'One thing is certain. Spend even a brief amount of time in Scott Morrison's company and you are left with the lasting impression that, while he believes God will always be in charge, he's nevertheless ready to lead.'

That same year, Morrison returned to social media after an absence of eighteen months. He went back to offering online encouragement to his football team, the Cronulla Sharks, and began posting photos of himself eating at restaurants serving food from other countries. The columnist Niki Savva wrote that some in the right wing of the Liberal Party believed Morrison would be the next prime minister, although he remained an unknown quantity to most voters. In a column describing him as having the potential to be 'the next John Howard, the most substantial conservative leader of his generation', she reported, with wry humour:

> A couple of weekends ago, with the same dedicated preparation as he showed in stopping the boats – clearly now on a mission to grab the votes – he cooked up a Sri Lankan fish curry and homemade chapattis for Annabel Crabb for an upcoming episode in her splendid TV series, *Kitchen Cabinet*. A delicious meal and a charming host sound like the perfect recipe for success. There appears no end to his talents.

Watching that episode of *Kitchen Cabinet* now, Morrison's public campaign to reinvent himself is obvious. In the first minutes of the show, Morrison outlines his chosen menu.

'These are your personal samosas – ScoMosa – recipe?' says the well-briefed Crabb.

'That's what my staff call them, yeah, the ScoMosas, everyone's getting used to this new nickname.'

Crabb then asks Morrison about something else new: 'You decided to start cooking earlier this year – what drove you to that?' Morrison says that with his new portfolio he is not travelling so much, and so tends to be around on weekends. Crabb tries her question again – why did he start cooking? – and Morrison talks about falling in love with Indian and Sri Lankan food on a trip to Sri Lanka for work. But that trip took place two years earlier. The answer is not obviously false, but nor is it obviously true.

The more important answer is clear enough. Morrison has found a way to mitigate the lingering sense of overt xenophobia that tends to attach to Liberal ministers for immigration. What better way to signal that the hardline, masculine immigration portfolio was behind him than to publicly embrace not only the gentler, traditionally female art of cooking, but the food of a people he had, not long ago, treated as unwelcome intruders?

But in doing this, Morrison has taken an unnecessary risk. To explain that we are now seeing the real Morrison, he has told us that the hardman was a role. He is, in other words, able to take on a particular demeanour, even a particular posture, when it suits his purposes. There is nothing to stop us assuming he is simply doing the same thing now.

This is a weakness in Crabb's argument. Even if we accept the truth of her proposition – that knowing what a politician is like can be powerful – there is no guarantee we will be able to glean this from her show, which, as critics pointed out at the time, was just one more staged presentation from a class of people masterful at staging their own public image.

But it is also true that you can learn something very valuable by watching that performance, if you are willing to give it your close attention. That Morrison is willing to turn other people's misfortune, and his role in that misfortune, into a stunt with which to advance his career – that he could go away to Sri Lanka, come back and ruin the lives of particular Sri Lankans, and then turn those experiences into an appealing quirk to be presented on national television – this seems an important measure of the man.

———

The problem of deciphering performance is not limited to television. It has been decades since Erving Goffman pointed out that we are all performing, in one way or another, all the time. The question *what is a person like* is hard to answer because it is hard to decide what is really being asked. Once we have peeled away the top layer, have we answered the question? Or after we have peeled the next layer away? How do we know when we have reached the final layer; how do we know if there even is a final layer?

These questions are unanswerable, but the reality of living is that we find a way to muddle through. We know, without really thinking about it, that when we meet somebody they are performing for us in various ways. We nevertheless assume that there is some way of reaching the real person behind the performance; real enough, anyway, to allow us to interact with them in a meaningful way.

And this, too, is what we do at an election, isn't it? Voters are very far from naive. They know they are watching a performance. In the ballot box, they ask themselves much the same set of questions we all ask, without really thinking about them, when we meet somebody new. Who do we think this person really is? Which parts of the performance should we pay attention to, and which should we ignore?

Just three years after *Kitchen Cabinet* aired, Scott Morrison became prime minister. Nine months after that, he won the federal election. In May 2019, three years of polling that showed Labor in front turned out to be a useless guide to what would happen. On election night, Morrison pronounced the result a miracle.

The shock victory was widely interpreted in a negative sense: as a rejection of the other candidate, Bill Shorten. He had offered too many policies, most of which seemed to be new taxes. He was an unpopular candidate, inauthentic and untrusted. The images he presented – of himself and of the country – found no traction.

There was some truth to this – but the idea that a particular election is a mere rejection of one candidate risks missing something crucial. To be elected prime minister, a candidate must first make their way through some of the nation's most powerful institutions. Then they must persuade a large number of voters. There is luck involved in this, of course, but the greatest luck of all is in the confluence of a particular person, with particular talents, facing the voters of a particular country at a particular time. Or to put this another way: if it is to succeed, the performance that person chooses to give – the performance they are able to give – must meet with a willing audience.

BLAMELESS

For a man who had just lost the most important job in the country, Malcolm Turnbull appeared in remarkably good humour. Standing in the grey and sheltered light of the Prime Minister's Courtyard for his final press conference, he joked a little, even smiled at times. Turnbull is a handsome, silver-haired man who has been a figure in Australian public life since his twenties. He has been a journalist, a businessman, a Rhodes scholar and a barrister. He is very rich and conspicuously articulate, with a patrician bearing and a grand accent. It was always expected that he would become prime minister, and once he had, great things were expected of his time in office. Instead, he had failed, more or less, and now his party had torn him down. Turnbull, though, seemed sanguine.

Often, a journalist will watch a politician speak and make the mistake of believing that something clear has been said. It is easy to attribute a certain authority to this person with a title and the words they have chosen; you instinctively absorb the prestige that has become attached to them and lend it to their sentences. Only afterwards, reading back over the transcript of the event, do you realise that phrases which had seemed quite reasonable only an hour beforehand are, in fact, mostly gibberish. Nothing interesting has been said,

nothing solid, nothing that is not a meaningless platitude or an incoherent mixture of thoughts that have little to do with one another.

Turnbull's final press conference was the opposite of that.
Afterwards, you could have walked away thinking that nothing
much had been said, convinced – by his smiles and his air of uncon-
cern – that what had just transpired was mildly unfortunate, nothing
more. It was only afterwards, reading his words on the page, that
the extent of Turnbull's bitterness became clear. He described the
events of the week as 'madness' and 'destructive action'. He was the
victim of 'a determined insurgency'. He twice mentioned disloy-
alty. His removal was the result of 'personal ambition' and – giving
a slightly Shakespearean air to proceedings – 'vengeance'.

Surprisingly, none of these dramatic words and phrases was
directed at Turnbull's successor. The new prime minister, Scott
Morrison, seemed to occupy very little of Turnbull's mind. He was
mentioned, but only, it seemed, on the way to other, more important matters. Turnbull thanked him for his 'great work' as a 'very
loyal and effective treasurer', and wished him 'the very best, of
course'. There was nothing either glowing or damning, no particularly heartfelt assertions, as you can tell from that 'of course'. The
Morrison section of Turnbull's monologue was pro forma.

That evening, this blameless afterthought took on the role that
Turnbull had lost, swearing, as a prime minister must, that he would
well and truly serve the people of Australia and bear true allegiance
to Queen Elizabeth II.

It is not clear when the obvious fact began to dawn on Turnbull:
that the man who had gained most from his removal might have
been instrumental in the events that led to it.

———

The move against Turnbull had been instigated by Peter Dutton, a former police officer from Queensland with a thin, bald head that some likened, with unkind accuracy, to a potato. He was an unsubtle man, given to blunt and broad assertions, who was detested by his critics on the left and who, in his time as immigration minister, was viewed as even more hardline than Morrison had been.

The Friday before, a story in *The Daily Telegraph*, Sydney's Murdoch tabloid, asserted that some conservative MPs were urging Dutton to take the leadership. Apparently, Dutton himself – who had never seemed a man given to searching indecision – was torn about what to do. The next day, on its front page, the *Telegraph* carried a new report: that Dutton had told those colleagues he would give serious thought to their proposal.

Turnbull had once worked for Australia's richest man, Kerry Packer, a slimy, charismatic bully of an impressive obesity that cartoonists loved to mock. When Packer had turned on him over a suspected leak, threatening to kill him, Turnbull told him that his assassin had better hit – because if he happened to miss, then Turnbull certainly wouldn't miss Packer. With age, Turnbull had become less patient still. The regular meeting of Liberal MPs at Parliament House was scheduled for Tuesday. A challenge to Turnbull's leadership was far from certain but was obviously a possibility. Rather than waiting to be ambushed, Turnbull, having given no sign during most of the meeting that anything out of the ordinary was going on, announced at its end that he would vacate his position. There would be an immediate vote for the position of prime minister.

Most MPs were stunned. Dutton was the only candidate to stand against Turnbull. He received thirty-five votes. Turnbull received forty-eight – which wasn't good enough. He had won, but the margin of victory was too small to give him the aura of invincibility a sitting prime minister needs. Several MPs concluded that his leadership was as good as over. After a very brief pause, the chaos within the Liberal Party continued. Turnbull decided to call another meeting, hoping to bring things to a head. The meeting did that, but this time Turnbull lost.

———

Unless you are obsessed by politics, questions of who voted for whom, and the precise numbers of votes each candidate received, are not usually very interesting. In attempting to understand Scott Morrison, they are essential. Afterwards, Morrison would claim that during the events that led to his taking over as prime minister, he was only a bystander; his ascent had happened entirely independent of his intentions.

Morrison says that he voted for Turnbull, and that is probably true. But no one becomes prime minister without followers, and the central question, in determining how a sufficient number of votes was gathered to ensure his victory, is: what did Morrison's followers do?

It is impossible to know for sure. But suspicions were raised by the way the numbers fell. On the Friday, there were two ballots. The first was a vote on whether to spill the Liberal leadership – that is, to declare that the leader was no longer leader and that anybody could now stand for the position. If this vote had gone Turnbull's way, then there would not have been a second vote and the crisis would have been over (at least for a while). Obviously, Turnbull wanted this vote to fail, and Dutton wanted it to succeed.

But the vote went against Turnbull. The leadership was now open, and the meeting moved on to the second vote. Having convinced enough MPs to vote with him, Dutton had good reason to be confident going into the second vote – the one to decide who would become Liberal leader and therefore prime minister. Turnbull chose not to stand, leaving Morrison, Dutton and the foreign minister, Julie Bishop, as candidates. In the first round of voting, Bishop was eliminated, leaving Dutton and Morrison. In the final round, Dutton lost to Morrison.

The point made by Morrison's critics was simple enough. In the first vote that day, forty-five MPs voted to declare the leadership open – as Dutton wanted them to – and forty voted against. In the second vote, that distribution reversed itself – forty-five MPs voted for Morrison, and forty voted for Dutton. Morrison's critics soon asked: if only forty people were in Dutton's corner, as the second vote made clear, why had forty-five people voted to spill the leadership? The only plausible answer was that Morrison's small gang of supporters must have voted with Dutton's supporters to remove Turnbull, knowing they could then switch sides to win the next vote for Morrison. Those critics had a further suggestion: that the same small gang had voted for Dutton against Turnbull on the Tuesday, too, in order to weaken Turnbull's leadership.

———

This was the position that Turnbull eventually reached. In his memoir, released almost two years later, Turnbull writes that during the events he did not believe that Morrison was working against him, because Morrison understood that Turnbull planned to retire before the next election, handing him the job. Then he writes:

> On the other hand, there's no doubt at least half-a-dozen of Scott's closest allies (and he didn't have a large number) voted for Dutton in the ballot on the Tuesday. The idea that they did that without his knowledge is fanciful. Scott is a control freak and I'd seen before in the ballots in 2015 how he'd publicly vote one way while ensuring his supporters voted the other way. So, regrettably, while it's never possible to be 100 per cent certain about these things, I have come to conclude Scott was playing a double game: professing public loyalty to me while at the same time allowing his supporters to undermine me.

That Morrison's supporters voted against Turnbull and then for Morrison did not guarantee there had been a conspiracy. Perhaps some MPs were sick of Turnbull, but, having got rid of him, and faced with two options, simply preferred Morrison to Dutton. Not long after the vote, one Morrison ally made exactly this argument to me. It is plausible, even likely, that Morrison did not tell anybody to vote a certain way. It is also true that Morrison gave Turnbull advice designed to save his prime ministership: that he should hold off calling the Friday spill. But the idea that Morrison bore no responsibility for Turnbull's removal rests on a presentation of

Morrison as either uninterested in what happened or powerless. The first idea is ridiculous, the second only slightly less so. Did he really not have sufficient authority over his supporters to say to them, 'Stop it, I want you to support Malcolm Turnbull, and that means voting against the spill'? He sounds a little like the crooked cop who looks the other way while the bank is being robbed, whistling innocently, knowing he'll get his cut soon enough.

Perhaps the most convincing account came from former Liberal MP Craig Laundy. It took a while to emerge. I spoke to Laundy a few weeks after the vote, well before the 2019 election. He would not go into the details of what had happened, saying only that while various theories were floating around, Morrison had been fighting by Turnbull's side until the fight was lost. But after the election, when his version of events stood no chance of jeopardising the party's chances, Laundy permitted the journalist David Crowe to publish his account of a meeting of Morrison's supporters on the Thursday afternoon just before the second spill:

> Name by name, [Morrison supporters Alex Hawke and Stuart Robert] read out a list of MPs and discussed how they thought they had voted in the secret ballot on Tuesday and how they might vote in a second challenge. Laundy found himself disagreeing over the names they claimed had voted for Dutton but would switch to Morrison. He told the group that one MP they mentioned was '100 per cent' with Turnbull on Tuesday. Robert disagreed with a smile. 'You've now worked out we haven't always been on the same team,' he said, in Laundy's account of this exchange.

Laundy fell silent. He pondered how this group could be so sure they had a cohort of MPs who would vote for Dutton in one ballot and move to Morrison a few days later. 'I felt sick in the guts,' he said later. 'It would be fair to say I was in shock.' He walked back to the Prime Minister's suite, entered [Turnbull's principal private secretary Sally] Cray's office, shut the door behind him and spoke: 'We've been played.'

———

What makes Turnbull's narrative of Morrison's betrayal so hard to resist is not Laundy's account but its resemblance to a series of events just three years earlier. In 2015, one prime minister had unexpectedly replaced another. The challenger then had been Turnbull, taking the prime ministership from the arch-conservative Tony Abbott.

After the vote, Morrison argued he had been loyal to Abbott until the end. In a technical sense, this was probably true – it seemed that Morrison had, as he claimed, voted for Abbott. But it was widely believed that Morrison's followers had voted for Turnbull, in order to bring in a new leader and secure Morrison's promotion to treasurer. It was, in effect, a dress rehearsal for what would happen three years later.

Turnbull makes much of this earlier chain of events in his memoir. In 2014, just a year after the Liberals won government, Morrison began to 'sniff out interest' in removing Abbott. More conversations took place – according to Turnbull – on the phone and over dinner. Finally, as his account nears the end of Abbott's leadership, Turnbull writes: 'Morrison was playing an audaciously duplicitous game, protesting publicly that he supported Abbott while busily working to bring him down.'

In telling this parallel story, Turnbull is working hard to lead us to the conclusion he has by now reached about his own removal. In these parts of the book, he returns to his training, donning his barrister's garb in order to gain the conviction he desires. A man is on the stand, accused of murder. There is no evidence directly connecting him to the crime; it is all circumstantial. But there is strong evidence suggesting that the man has killed before, not that long ago, using precisely the same techniques. If Turnbull can convince us of this earlier crime, then we will likely believe him about the more recent one too.

At one point, Turnbull writes about Morrison saying that he cannot vote against Abbott: 'Hypocrisy dripping from every syllable.' This is a diary entry, and so we can (probably) take it as an accurate rendering of Turnbull's perception of Morrison in that moment. But Turnbull is writing his memoir much later, and with a more considered purpose than merely noting down events. Like any skilled writer, Turnbull is selecting from the material in front of him to tell the story that he wants to tell. Elsewhere, Turnbull includes a text message Morrison had sent him just after Morrison had taken the job:

As Morrison was sworn in on Friday evening, I messaged him. 'Congratulations Prime Minister, and good luck!' He replied the next morning.

'Only you can know how I feel today, but I cannot begin to know how you feel. I loved working for and with you. I'm really proud of what we did. And that is always how I will always feel and speak of it. I want you to know I am thinking about you a great deal and you know I pray for you. That doesn't change now. I don't know why all this happened, but now it has come upon me, you know I will be relying on my faith, friends and values to overcome and conquer what is ahead . . . Thank you for all you've done for me. But above all as one PM to another, thank you for everything you did for our country. No one knows that contribution better than me. Love you mate.'

I replied, 'You too Scomo!'

The inclusion of this message seems designed to illustrate two facts. The first is Turnbull's easy grace at a time of personal disappointment. The second is Morrison's insincerity, his queasy willingness to say things that cannot, once you know the full story, possibly ring true.

———

There is one element of Turnbull's story that is unconvincing. Given his detailed knowledge of Morrison's treachery towards Abbott, you might expect Turnbull to have realised that at some point Morrison would come for him. Others certainly did: Turnbull writes that 'everybody told me not to trust Morrison'. Instead, he put 'great trust' in his treasurer.

Why didn't Turnbull listen to his colleagues? The answer is in three parts.

The first he offers in the book: that he wanted to get things done and could not afford to descend into a paranoid fog. This might be true, but it is also silly – to watch a colleague stab a leader in the back and refuse to believe he will do the same to you is embarrassingly naive. But then Turnbull was often naive when it came to politics – this is the second factor.

The third part of the answer lies with Morrison. Turnbull writes that he trusted his treasurer. But there is trust and there is trust; all of us trust people, every day, whom we don't really know. We trust strangers to drive on the correct side of the road, and doctors and banks with our secrets. The type of trust that exists at an emotional level is of a different order. When this trust is betrayed – when a lover cheats or a good friend suddenly turns cold – we find it wrenching. If Turnbull and Morrison were really friends, if Turnbull had sincerely placed great trust in Morrison, you might have expected some of this emotion to find its way into the writing. Instead, there is something bloodless about Turnbull's descriptions of Morrison's behaviour; he can be direct, even mildly lyrical ('dripping from every syllable'), but the prose never takes on the tone of genuine hurt.

This distinction becomes obvious in Turnbull's writing about another of his senior ministers, Mathias Cormann, who was central to Dutton's efforts to remove Turnbull. Here, Turnbull is willing to use the word 'betrayal', a word he never uses in referring to Morrison. He writes that 'Cormann's treachery was the worst and the most hurtful'. The wound was still open when he wrote these pages, as you can tell from this spiteful passage, which made me exclaim when I read it for the first time:

He'd become a trusted friend of mine, and of Lucy as I've described above. He used to send me pictures of his children and on occasion asked me to pose for photos with his daughter when she visited him in Canberra. On 10 July, he sent one of those pictures to Lucy with the message, 'Lucy had to share this with you too. Great catch up for my five year old with Malcolm today. Will be very meaningful to her as she gets older . . .' Indeed it will be.

About Cormann, Turnbull's writing has the plainness and clarity of pain. He is angry. When he writes about Morrison, his personal criticisms are offhand, witty flourishes; amusing slights. He is frustrated by what happened to him, amazed that this ordinary man has bested him. But he does not feel betrayed, because you can only be betrayed by somebody who has convinced you that they care for you – and this is only possible if you feel you have seen inside that person.

Perhaps this is why Turnbull did not see Morrison coming. We respond to people not on the basis of logic but of instinct. There are certain people who provoke suspicion and others who don't. Suspicion depends on attention. Those who make us suspicious have made us notice them; we begin to watch them, to monitor them for signs of deception. They get into our heads, become objects of obsession. We are suspicious of them not because we don't know what they are thinking, but because we believe we know exactly what they're thinking.

But there was something about Morrison that deflected the attentive gaze; that prevented Turnbull, an intelligent man with an observant eye, from looking at him too intently. There is a sense, in Turnbull's book – as in his final press conference – that Morrison, as a living soul, as a person beyond the job that he was doing, never quite came into focus for him.

AUTHENTIC

In September 2018, less than two weeks after the events that made him prime minister, Scott Morrison was interviewed on breakfast television from a rugby league stadium, the goalposts clearly visible behind him. He said that it had been 'a confusing and bewildering series of events, and not ones that I had any part in'. Asked about the theory he had somehow orchestrated the events leading up to his leadership, he said that if that was true, then 'Elvis is cutting hair in Lithgow'. Then he declared that the previous era was over: 'The curtain's come down on that Muppet Show and an absolute new curtain has lifted up.'

Immediately after he took over, the Liberal vote fell sharply; Labor's vote rose even more sharply. A question asked at every poll, separate from the question of which way voters will vote, is which of the prime minister and the Opposition leader they think should be in the top job. Suddenly, with Turnbull's downfall and Morrison's rise, the leader of the Labor Party, Bill Shorten, was the nation's preferred leader. It was the first time this had happened in three years.

This was not surprising. Shorten was not well liked, but Morrison was the most anonymous politician to become prime minister in several decades. Bob Hawke had been a famous union leader for years. Paul Keating had been Hawke's treasurer for eight years. John Howard had been a senior MP for decades, and held the second-most prominent political job – Opposition leader – twice. Kevin Rudd, via breakfast television, had turned himself into a new kind of political celebrity, and had been Opposition leader. Julia Gillard had been deputy prime minister, and the first woman in that role. She was beaten by Tony Abbott, who had been Opposition leader for four years and two elections. Abbott was replaced by Turnbull. And then came Morrison.

It was not only Turnbull who had failed to fix his gaze on this new leader. Despite his three years as treasurer, Morrison had somehow failed to leave much of an impression on Australians. In September, approaching the Melbourne Cricket Ground, he was caught on camera as he stopped to shake hands with a Geelong supporter. The man had a question for him: 'What's your name, then?' Newspapers across the country ran brief biographies to catch their readers up, under the heading 'Who is Scott Morrison?'.

Morrison set about answering the question. A week after he became prime minister, he gave his first one-on-one interview to a newspaper, for the Murdoch tabloids printed in most of the nation's capital cities. He said, of that first week in power, 'Two major things didn't happen, I didn't get my footy tips in on Thursday night and I am not going to get to cook a curry tonight.'

There is nothing unusual in a politician talking about their hobbies. In 2019, when he was not yet prime minister of the United Kingdom but seemed certain to be soon, Boris Johnson, sitting on a fine white sofa in front of a grand wooden fireplace, was asked what he did to switch off. Looking away from the interviewer with a wistful expression, he said, 'I like to paint.' Then, with the smallest of smiles on his lips, he said, 'I make things.' Asked what things, he said he made buses – models of buses, constructed from cardboard boxes. Then he painted passengers, enjoying themselves. Johnson delivered all of this quite slowly, haltingly, waving his hands through the air as though to help him visualise what he was saying. It seemed as though he might be making it up, just to see how far he could push things. There was speculation at the time to that effect – Johnson has a long history of making things up. The video was widely shared online, as something to laugh at. But in the brief burst of analysis afterwards, evidence emerged to suggest Johnson had been painting boxes in his private time for years – he had once painted a picture of his family visiting the Colosseum – and had recently turned his illustrative attention to London's most famous form of transport.

Johnson's hobby was eccentric; Morrison's was ordinary. What stands out is not its nature but just how often he managed to bring it up. This began just before he took the job. As he walked into the room where the vote for a new prime minister would be conducted, he told the media: 'The only tip I've got – Sharks to beat Newcastle this weekend.' In his first prime ministerial press conference, a few hours later, he said – in an odd combination of humour, football and refugee policy – 'We all want to be able to make our own choices in life. Whether it's about who comes to our country, as John Howard famously said, or what school you want your kids to go to, or what team they want to follow – I suggest the Sharks.'

It is possible to be too cynical. Sometimes politicians are just making dumb jokes. Morrison's contrivance, though, was extreme.

The very first TV interview he gave as prime minister was not to a political journalist or even a breakfast television host, but to a rugby league star. One of the first videos produced by his press team was a montage of twenty times he had said 'Go Sharks!' or something similar. In his first week as leader, he gave a press conference while holding a rugby league ball. In September, he gave an interview to Sabra Lane, host of the ABC's flagship radio current affairs program, *AM*. The topics were schools funding, Papua New Guinea, aged care, and the obstacles to women succeeding in the Liberal Party. Morrison concluded the interview, with no context and no lead-up, like this: 'Thanks a lot, Sabra. Great to be here. Go the Sharks.'

––––––

Morrison's personal standing did not take long to rise in the polls. He was behind Shorten just once as preferred prime minister; at the Newspoll immediately after that, he took the lead. At the poll after that, in late September, he increased his lead, and the Liberal vote began to rise.

In that late-September poll, another question was asked: which leader did voters believe was most authentic? This term, *authentic*, was defined as somebody genuine or true to their beliefs. The answers to this question allowed Simon Benson at *The Australian*, which had commissioned the poll, to write that Morrison had emerged 'as a more trusted and authentic leader' than Shorten.

News like this can take hold quickly, if encouraged by the right people. *The Australian* is read by the political class. Benson's Newspoll copy would have been read by every political journalist and every politician, and so, unsurprisingly, the point about authenticity was picked up and repeated by other political journalists. Later that day, on Sky News – which, much like *The Australian*, was followed in every political office in Parliament House – Liberal minister Alan Tudge said, 'I just think that Scott is a very authentic individual.'

Three weeks later another Newspoll was released. Responding to the results, cabinet minister Simon Birmingham said the prime minister had done an 'incredible job over the past couple of months connecting with voters across Australia . . . He's seen as authentic.' In November, the former New South Wales police commissioner, a friend of Morrison, described him as 'genuine, authentic and courageous. My impressions are not of the politician, they are of the man. He's a very genuine Australian . . . an honest, forthright man, exactly what you'd want, and we want more genuine, authentic, courageous leaders.' A few weeks after that, John Howard, Morrison's hero and mentor, who spoke regularly to Morrison, said, 'He's come across to the Australian people as an authentic, genuine, direct person.'

It is worth noting that the initial Newspoll did not find that voters saw Morrison as authentic. It showed that voters found him more authentic than Shorten – and in fact, still less than half the population believed him more authentic than Shorten, with a significant portion, we can assume, undecided.

The word 'authentic' had not come out of nowhere. Two weeks before the Newspoll story, the prime minister himself had told the parliament, 'As a new prime minister, I understand I have a big job to do as I demonstrate to Australians my authenticity.' Morrison had, in effect, constructed his own test. The polling, conducted for and reported by a newspaper favourably disposed to Morrison, appeared to confirm that he had passed it. Then his colleagues, friends and mentor affirmed this, and their words were broadcast and printed across the land.

Political outsiders might see efficient conspiracy in this. Those who have been on the inside know that politics is rarely quite that organised. Still, conversations are had in certain circles; suggestions are made by powerful individuals. The only thing more naive than believing that the fate of the world is decided by two or three men in a smoky room is believing that there is no truth at all in that image – that the dissemination of certain concepts and ideas through the public sphere, and from there through a society, is entirely accidental.

———

Morrison had been contemplating the idea of authenticity for some time. In 2017, still a year away from becoming prime minister, he delivered a speech to a meeting of the Liberal Party. He spoke of entrenched cynicism and a disconnected electorate. 'To crack through this thick ice,' Morrison said, 'we must communicate candidly and with authenticity.' He cited Donald Trump and British Labour leader Jeremy Corbyn as politicians who had taken on 'the role of the authentic outsider; the one to challenge a system that voters did not think was serving them'.

Once Morrison became prime minister, he set about following his own advice, by performatively challenging that system. He began by distancing himself from the party that he led, calling it a 'Muppet Show'. Not long afterwards, he cancelled a scheduled meeting with the premiers, and when asked about it said, 'The only thing that happens as a result of not having that COAG meeting is less Tim Tams will be consumed in Canberra that week.' In an interview with right-wing radio host Alan Jones, he segued into an attack on global institutions: 'I'm not going to spend money on global climate conferences and all that sort of nonsense.' Within weeks of taking over as leader, he had ridiculed government at a state, national and international level. He was – with his rhetoric – challenging a system that voters did not think was serving them, and presenting himself as 'the authentic outsider'.

A still more illuminating comment was made outside the 2017 speech to the Liberal Party. In an interview to promote the event, with Sharri Markson at *The Daily Telegraph*, Morrison said that 'the staged nature of politics' had been the orthodoxy for a long time, but 'that's not the way forward anymore. People are looking for a more honest, direct engagement. They're interested in what you think about the footy or what you cook because that's their life, that's what they talk about.'

It is remarkable how accurately this laid out the strategy Morrison adopted once he became leader. Immediately, he made sure that voters knew exactly what he thought about the footy and exactly what he cooked.

———

Morrison's love of the Cronulla Sharks seems sincere – or, at least, not insincere. He very often watches them play. The team's chairman has said that, when he does, he is focused and concentrated, and when the weather is bad, he declines the chance to sit in the glass-walled viewing areas. *The Footy Show* has aired footage of Morrison kicking a goal – he does it quite easily – at Shark Park, the local football stadium. And this sincerity has been accepted. A detailed survey of Morrison's career in *The Australian Financial Review*, introducing the new prime minister to its readers, concluded like this: 'A move to The Lodge in Yarralumla is on the cards, but don't even think about asking him to start barracking for the Canberra Raiders.'

This was a cute ending – except that Morrison had already changed teams once, and changed football codes as well. A 2006 CV emerged in one of Niki Savva's columns, listing Morrison's old interests. Rugby league was not mentioned – in fact, it was the only one of Australia's three major codes not to be included. He had started out as a rugby union man. The divide between the two codes in Sydney is sharp: rich private-school kids follow rugby union, often just called 'rugby', while working-class kids follow rugby league.

The CV also mentioned Australian Rules, and the team that Morrison supported, the Western Bulldogs. He tweeted about the Bulldogs several times during the finals in both 2009 and 2010 – he was singing the club song. Asked on Twitter why he had chosen the Dogs, he said he liked their coach, and that 'loyalty counts'.

A decade later, in April 2019, Morrison told a Melbourne radio host that he didn't have an AFL team:

> I like AFL but I am not a phoney. I am not going to go around pretending I am something I am not. I grew up in New South Wales, a suburban boy. I've been following that code ever since

I was a kid. I am who I am. I like going, I really enjoy it. But
when I back something, I'm all in. So I follow my team, which
is the Sharks and the Southern District Rebels up there in the
Sydney comp . . . I am never going to be someone I am not. I
am not going to be inauthentic. What you see is what you get.

The issue is trivial: nobody really cares which football code or
team a politician follows; despite what Australians like to tell
themselves, nobody cares, either, that a politician has switched
allegiances, and Morrison is not the first prime minister to have
done so. It is this triviality that makes the vehemence of Morrison's
response so telling.

The radio discussion began after Morrison had used an analogy
about a player for Collingwood. The interviewer playfully suggested Morrison was jumping on the Collingwood bandwagon.
Immediately, the prime minister spoke over him, saying twice, 'I
don't have a team.' This was odd enough – it was only banter. But
then Morrison did what he had done in the Hadley interview about
the funerals: defensively, he began to speak at length about himself.
Over and over, in different words, he made the same point: *I'm not
a phoney, I won't pretend to be something I'm not, I am who I am, when
I back something I'm all in, I am never going to be someone I am not, I'm
not going to be inauthentic.*

It was a striking display, strangely defensive, comprehensively
rejecting an accusation that had not really been made, and certainly
not with any seriousness. It is difficult, at first, to understand what
might have sparked it – until you realise that Morrison could not
afford to have the charge stick because of how close to the truth

it ran. He was pretending to be something he wasn't; when he backed something – like, say, the Western Bulldogs – he was not all in, but, rather, entirely willing to give it up and then deny that it had ever happened. Even the most apparently innocent assertion of fact in this short passage was more shadowy than it seemed. When Morrison said, 'I've been following that code ever since I was a kid,' he was implying he had always followed rugby league, whereas in fact the code he had always followed was rugby union.

At this point, the election was a month away.

———

The novelist Ford Madox Ford admired this sentence, from Maupassant: 'He was a gentleman with red whiskers who always went first through a doorway.' Ford wrote: '[T]hat gentleman is so sufficiently got in that you need no more of him to understand how he will act. He has been "got in" and can get to work at once.' The novelist and critic James Wood, in his modern classic *How Fiction Works*, quotes these sentences and observes: 'Very few brushstrokes are needed to get a portrait walking, as it were.'

I can easily imagine Morrison as that gentleman with red whiskers, always going first through doorways. But instead of those few brushstrokes, Morrison gave us others: he cooked a curry once a week – just once – and liked rugby league. So few details, but such talkative details! They told us that he loved his family and made sure he had time to spend with them; he was modern, because he knew how to cook; but he only cooked once a week, because he was still a real man, with traditional values and an important job. He embraced multiculturalism in the way that Australians have always embraced multiculturalism: by loving other people's food. He was a man who identified with, or at least understood, the working class, whose football code he had adopted. Finally, he was a man who loved his neighbourhood. Together, these personal details signalled that he was authentic, true to himself, honest – partly because he told us this was what they signalled, and partly because he convinced enough of the press to report the same thing.

Ford and Wood were talking about characters, and Morrison is a real person – but the distinction is not as meaningful as it might at first seem. In the late 1980s, the journalist Janet Malcolm interviewed a psychiatrist who had testified, at trial, on the personality of a murderer. The psychiatrist had never met the murderer. Instead, he had read a book about the murders, and reviewed a 600-page transcript of thirty tape recordings the murderer had created while in prison. On this basis, he testified that the man suffered from 'malignant narcissism'. So convinced was the psychiatrist of his judgement that he told Malcolm, 'I was highly nervous about being in the presence of this man . . . I made a point of finding out when he would be paroled, and when I learned that it was after the time I would no longer be on earth I felt bolder.' Malcolm replied, 'You talk about him as if you really knew him, as if he were a real person. But actually he's a character in a book. Everything we know about him we know from [the book].'

Something similar could be said of voters and their impressions of the people who represent them. What do we know of the politicians of whom, between elections, we express both broad and specific judgements, and whom we then judge again, with finality, at the election itself? Only what we are told by the people who craft the news bulletins that we watch and listen to, and who write the articles that we read. To us, these politicians are not much different from the characters we read about in books.

In his Clark lectures, delivered at Cambridge College in 1927, the novelist E.M. Forster put forward a theory of literary characters. There were two sorts: flat characters and round characters. Flat characters were sometimes called 'types' or 'caricatures', and were constructed around a single idea or quality. They could be described simply, captured in a sentence or two. Often they would have a catchphrase. One of the advantages of a flat character for the novelist, Forster said, was that they never needed reintroducing, because they were so easily recognised.

Isn't this a fine description of Morrison? When he became prime minister, we did not know much about him. Quickly, he set about helping us to know him, by making himself a flat character. We were given just a few details; we were given them over and over again. These details gave us clues to other parts of his character, but, crucially, none that complicated the portrait. Instead, they confirmed each other, leaving us with a man who could be described in a few phrases. Here, for example, are the first paragraphs of a brief column about Morrison published in the tabloid newspapers the day after he became prime minister:

> Scott Morrison follows Paul Keating and John Howard as treasurers elevated to the office of prime minister.
>
> And like Howard, Morrison is the epitome of middle-Australia – it doesn't get more suburban than the Shire.
>
> He's a daggy dad. He loves his footy team, the Sharks.

He eats meat pies – not with a knife and fork – and has his mates over for a barbecue.

The details of the description – even the fact that he loves the Sharks – are not the most important thing. The reason this description works so well is not because it conjures details. Quite the opposite: it is because it conjures a type. He is 'the epitome of middle-Australia', the good bloke down the road. If, after a month of this, voters felt they knew who Morrison was enough to trust him, it was not because they knew Morrison as a man, but as a type; and they had known that type all their lives.

Morrison had demonstrated a certain skill in creating this flat character. But this skill would have been useless without another, which preceded it. Not far into Morrison's prime ministership, veteran journalist Michelle Grattan quoted a Labor man arguing that the contest now was about trying to define Morrison. 'The prime minister is a blank canvas,' he said. That a man who had been in politics for ten years and in public life for twenty could have remained a 'blank canvas' for so long was as necessary to the emergence of 'ScoMo' as the Sharks and the curries themselves.

PRAGMATIC

Two weeks after Scott Morrison became prime minister, Joshua Gane posted on Facebook that he had been driving to the Queensland coast with a friend when the friend bit through a strawberry and swallowed half a sewing needle. They checked the other strawberries and found another needle. Now he was posting from hospital, where they had taken his friend, who was suffering from severe abdominal pain.

Soon, there were other reports of strawberry tampering – around a hundred. Some reports turned out to be false but there were plenty of genuine cases, with perpetrators copying the crime they'd read about. Seven days after Gane's friend swallowed half a needle, Morrison and his health minister held a press conference. A question was asked about the strawberries, but Morrison felt no need to say anything, and let his minister answer.

The next day, Scott Morrison met with Pauline Hanson, leader of the far-right party One Nation, who called for the government to give money to strawberry farmers, whom she described as 'the victims of an act of terror'.

Two days after that, Morrison held another press conference. He distanced himself from Hanson's comments, while doing what she had suggested and making much the same point: 'What you get fifteen years for are things like possessing child pornography and financing terrorism – that's how seriously I take this.'

The announcement Morrison made had only a little substance. There were already criminal penalties – Morrison said there would be a small increase to the prison sentence, along with a change to the legal definition of 'sabotage' and a new offence of 'recklessness'. The show around the announcement, though, was huge. It was a legitimate issue. 'But,' wrote Michelle Grattan, 'when the government rolls out the Prime Minister, the Attorney-General, the Home Affairs Minister, the Australian Federal Police chief and the Border Force Commissioner, and then rushes new legislation through parliament in a single day – well, you know a political point is being made. A serious crime was turned into a national crisis.'

Soon, Morrison tweeted out his suggestion that people make a pavlova with strawberries that weekend to support the farmers. The next morning he said on breakfast TV that Jen would make a 'pav' and he would make a curry. He talked to FM radio hosts Fitzy and Wippa, ate strawberries for their listeners and made a Sharks reference. A serious crime had been turned into a national crisis; in turn, a national crisis had been turned into a chance to strengthen Morrison's image as a curry-cooking, Sharks-loving family man.

————

That week had been busy. Along with the strawberry penalties, Morrison had announced a quick fix to a controversial school funding issue, and loosened rules so that hay trucks could more quickly get feed to cattle. He had announced a summit (on the drought) and an inquiry (into aged care), and asked his party – after allegations of bullying arose – to consider what steps it would take to establish an internal complaints process.

These were all political fixes rather than detailed, considered policy decisions – in fact three were not policy announcements at all, but only promises to make policy announcements sometime in the future. But together they provided a political fix to another problem: the government's complete lack of a policy agenda. In the Senate that week, the government insisted on debating bills that already had bipartisan support, just so that parliament would have something to do. When Labor tried to force a vote on one of these issues, the government blocked the vote so the pointless debate could continue. But Morrison had found a way to direct the attention of the media elsewhere, with the prime minister having promised the new strawberry laws would pass the parliament that week. As one journalist noted:

> The story that sums up the Morrison government's haste to look like they're getting things done is the journey the strawberry legislation had to take.
>
> In order to make the new penalties law, the documents had to be flown to Darwin, where Governor-General Sir Peter Cosgrove is visiting a school in Humpty Doo.
>
> The government jet will fly an 8000km round trip with the papers to get his signature so they can become law this week.

Morrison's propensity to put on a show was registered; for some journalists, this provoked scepticism. But another narrative was being built, at the same time, around the same actions. Dennis Shanahan at *The Australian* – the only national broadsheet, and owned, like the tabloids, by Rupert Murdoch – praised the government's tactical skill, and wrote that Morrison could 'switch from vaudeville to serious policy decisions and political problem-solving while not taking his eyes off Labor'. In another column, he wrote that the strawberry announcement had provided an answer to the question of why the party had had to replace Turnbull: Morrison was 'an ordinary leader talking about ordinary issues'. Graham Richardson – whom Cadzow had quoted, years earlier, in praise of Morrison – wrote much the same, also in *The Australian*: 'Morrison knows what the punters are thinking and on Wednesday his Twitter feed contained brilliance. He encapsulated everything ordinary folk think about the bastards sticking pins in strawberries and he put it in language that everyday people use.' In a third column by Shanahan that week, he wrote: 'With his down-to-earth language and image, Morrison is earning respect from critics.'

So Morrison was ordinary – and this was an advantage. He moved fast, jumping from one thing to another, and this was an advantage too. There was a third conclusion, offered by David Speers in the tabloids:

This prime minister is already proving to be a more pragmatic leader than his two immediate predecessors, determined to make faster decisions. Whether it was the royal commission into aged care, the tougher jail terms for sticking needles in strawberries or reaching a truce with the Catholic school sector, Morrison has swung into 'action man' mode.

This idea of Morrison as 'pragmatic' is significant, because by now it is an established part of the way journalists write about him. Before he took the job and during his early prime ministership, this apparent pragmatism was treated almost uniformly as a good thing. In March 2018, a few months before Morrison became prime minister, veteran journalist Paul Kelly wrote in *The Australian*: 'Morrison won't be intimidated. He sees himself as a practical "can-do" Treasurer who refuses to be intimidated by interests, ideology or orthodoxy.' Sharri Markson wrote in the tabloids in August 2019: 'Morrison has also cultivated a very clear identity as champion of middle Australia. It's for this group of voters that Morrison is governing and he has their image in mind when he announces policy, whether it's his practical, not ideological, approach to environmental policy, or tax reform.'

Would it surprise you to learn that Morrison had been the first to make this case for himself? In late 2014, in a long interview, Morrison described himself as a 'fixer', and said, about economic reform, 'I am a pragmatist on these issues, not an ideologue . . . the real indicator of the policy effect is what the results are going to be – not whether this one or that one was done.' A few months after that, not long after moving from immigration to social services, he said, 'I'm trying to solve the problem. I'm not wedded ideologically to any particular one of these measures.' Asked about welfare groups being surprised by how easy he was to work with, Morrison said, 'If they had had a misconception previously, what

I've always tried to do – in whatever role I've been in – is I'm there to try and fix a problem.' In an interview with the ABC a month after that, Morrison was asked whether the government would be bold on reform. 'Well, what we'll be is practical,' he said, before going on to say 'practical' four more times, and 'pragmatic' once.

When he became treasurer, the department website described 'Scott Morrison, or ScoMo' as 'a proven fixer'. And in 2017, a year before he became prime minister, he presented his budget as 'practical', repeating the word in interviews as a characterisation of both the budget and himself. 'I'm just quite a practical person,' he told the ABC's youth radio station Triple J. 'I think you've got to be pragmatic to get things done.'

This is vacuous language. An electrician can be practical, because his goal is obvious: keep the lights on. But the phrase 'I think you've got to be pragmatic to get things done' tells us nothing we might want to know about Morrison the politician, which comes down to a question he never answers: what exactly *are* these things he wants to get done? To 'fix' something sounds useful, because it implies that something is broken, which is readily verifiable if you are a plumber. But in politics, what is broken and what is not is very often a matter of opinion – in fact, it's pretty much the whole shebang, a massive part of what differentiates one prime minister from another. That Morrison could become prime minister with few notable achievements behind him, his most famous trait being that he supported a particular rugby league team, suggests that he had not, in his five years as a senior minister in the government, come across many things he considered broken.

———

Malcolm Turnbull had tried the same 'pragmatic' line, though with far less doggedness than Morrison. In December 2016, Turnbull said, 'You've got to be true to yourself . . . I am who I am. I'm a practical, pragmatic leader, I'm not an ideological leader. I'm determined to get the right outcomes, the great opportunities for Australians.'

This was an attempt to put another frame around the narrative that had, by then, already taken hold: that Turnbull was a weak prime minister who repeatedly gave in to the arch-conservatives in his party, unwilling to stand up for what he believed. Turnbull's great error had been to stand up for things earlier in his life. He gained a large part of his fame as the head of the republican movement. In his first stint as leader of the Liberal Party, in Opposition, he became known as a climate change warrior. Both these nationally prominent battles were famously lost, which only enhanced Turnbull's reputation as a man of strong and specific beliefs, willing to fight even if the cause was not popular.

Then, as prime minister, Turnbull abandoned those beliefs. His party was not interested in either issue, so he decided he was not that interested either. Voters felt betrayed, less because of the specific issues – public opinion was not monolithic on either – but because he was not the person he had held himself out to be. By the time he decided he was 'pragmatic', it was too late.

Morrison had the good sense never to make the mistake of attaching himself to clear beliefs. The most famous story about Morrison within the Liberal Party, before he became prime minister, concerned the party conference. Every few years, members of the party from all over the country meet to discuss policy and cheer the leader. Each time, there are separate dinners: one for the conservative faction and one for the moderate faction. The enmities within parties are often as great as those between parties; the faction with which you align yourself and the dinner you attend are deeply felt matters. That year, Morrison arrived late to the dinner for moderate Liberals. The senior MP George Brandis was speaking, and interrupted his speech to say to Morrison, 'So, which dinner have you just come from?' Morrison's occasional mentor, Bruce Baird, who was there, told me, 'Everyone laughed, and most people guessed.' According to Liberal Party legend, Morrison had come straight from the conservatives' dinner.

Several of Morrison's announcements, in that busy September week in 2018, were complete reversals of positions he had previously held. David Speers, in the same column in which he described Morrison as 'pragmatic', wrote: 'Labor, quite understandably, points out the hypocrisy each time a policy is reversed . . . But Morrison appears unfazed.'

This was not a new phenomenon. In 2017, as treasurer, Morrison announced he would be increasing the Medicare levy to fund the National Disability Insurance Scheme. Explaining the increase in a post-budget speech, he warned his audience he might become emotional: 'Forgive me as I try to get through this.' This made sense – he was talking, in part, about his wife's brother, Gary, who suffers from multiple sclerosis: 'I'm not saying no to Gary and the 500,000 Australians counting on this.'

A year later – after Labor had blocked efforts to impose the levy on lower-income earners – Morrison articulated a new position. The strong economy meant the levy hike was no longer needed.

He had talked to Gary. 'I spoke to him last night and he is very pleased – Gary did not want to see people pay more taxes either.'

––––––

This constant shifting from one position to another, along with Morrison's refusal to explain such shifts in a way that might reveal what he thought, were not the only methods he used to avoid being pinned down.

All politicians find ways to dodge their interrogators. A survey of this aspect of Morrison's career nonetheless manages to shock. A maxim of media training – one I've spouted myself, in my days as a press secretary to politicians, and one that has helped ruin interviews everywhere forever – is 'answer the question you wish you'd been asked'. Morrison, often, has not even bothered to appear to answer. He simply refuses to provide information, or keeps his answers so clipped as to be meaningless.

Journalists who watched Morrison closely as immigration minister became frustrated. Two of the most senior – Laurie Oakes, then political editor of Channel Nine, and David Marr, then with *The Guardian* – have described his approach with a similar level of obscenity. Oakes, at the time Morrison was immigration minister, said his 'disgusting' attitude amounted to him giving journalists 'the finger'. Marr, years later, wrote:

I remember the horrible press conferences he held as Minister for Immigration to beat up on the invasion of Australia by criminal hordes of asylum seekers. Beside him as a most uncomfortable piece of set decoration was General Angus

Campbell. Neither man answered a single question that
mattered.

What remains with me most vividly from that time was
Morrison's smile as he refused to play ball. A smile is a valuable thing in politics; a good, easy smile is a vote-winner. But
as he wouldn't say how many boats had been caught or how
many refugees had drowned on the way, Morrison's smile was
a little smile of victory: I'm not telling and you can't make
me. It said: fuck off.

Morrison's period in immigration was when this habit became
obvious. Before he took the job, the arrival of each boat carrying asylum seekers had been announced by his department. He
scrapped these announcements and replaced them with a weekly
briefing. Then he scrapped the weekly briefing and replaced it with
a weekly statement on paper. News that a boat had arrived might
only emerge days later, and without the chance for journalists to
ask the minister questions about it.

But before things reached that ridiculous stage, there was an
earlier ridiculous stage. Morrison had instituted an innovative pro-
tocol, one which would become mildly famous. No comment would
be provided, either by him or by the defence forces, about 'on-water
matters'. Refusing to answer questions about 'on-water matters',
for a minister whose most prominent job description was 'stopping
the boats', was a stunningly broad rejection of accountability.

Not that Morrison really needed the innovation: his press conferences were utterly absurd performances already. Consider this,
from November 2013:

QUESTION: But in terms of making a judgement, if those asylum seekers do come to Australia doesn't that mean your 'turn back the boats' policy is kind of . . .

MORRISON: Well, you've made a whole bunch of presumptions there which I'm not about to speculate on.

QUESTION: Well, maybe you can clear them up for us?

MORRISON: Well, you're the one making the presumptions, not me.

Seven months later, Morrison had perfected his technique. The transcripts of his press conferences are literally incredible; they have to be read to be believed, and even then you struggle. They are so strange – like a cross between Jorge Luis Borges and Joseph Heller.

The following three excerpts are taken from one long press conference in June 2014:

QUESTION: Minister is there a boat in trouble off Christmas Island?

MORRISON: It is our standard practice as you know under Operation Sovereign Borders to report on any significant events regarding maritime operations at sea particularly where there are safety of life at sea issues associated and I am advised I have no such reports to provide.

QUESTION: Is there a boat?

MORRISON: Well, I have answered the question.

QUESTION: But in terms, I guess the question is . . .

MORRISON: You are very well aware of what the Operation Sovereign Borders practice is regarding commentary on maritime operations and I do not intend to depart from the policies that we have been pursuing now since we have come to government. I remind you that these policies have been extremely successful and I am not about to depart from a successful approach.

*

QUESTION: Have you ever held talks with the Indian government about what to do in situations where a boat might come from India?

MORRISON: Well, I am not going to speculate on hypotheticals . . .

QUESTION: No, it is a question about what you may have done in the past. Have you ever envisioned the possibility of a boat coming from India?

MORRISON: It is Operation Sovereign Borders practice to engage with any such countries we may need to engage with in relation to our operations.

QUESTION: Have you done that with India?

MORRISON: I don't comment on the specifics of those things, I simply don't do it.

QUESTION: Mr Morrison, is this boat being towed back to India?

MORRISON: I have covered that issue, my response to that issue has been provided.

QUESTION: So, Mr Morrison, you are not even going to confirm there is a boat, you are not going to say what is happening, if people are in the water? Their boat is leaking, we are being told – leaking oil – and you are not going to say anything about that situation?

MORRISON: What I have said is that it is our practice to report on significant events at sea, particularly where they involve safety of life at sea. Now there is no such report for me to provide to you today. If there was a significant event happening then I would be reporting on it.

QUESTION: So what does that mean?

MORRISON: You are a bright journalist, I am sure you can work it out.

QUESTION: No, we are asking you, sir, you are the Minister.

MORRISON: And I have given you my response.

QUESTION: Yeah, why are you having a press conference if you are not here to reveal . . .

MORRISON: I am on my way in to the Federal Council and I was happy to provide a doorstop because I understood journalists had questions today.

QUESTION: So could you clarify, sir, for us: at what point does an event become a significant event involving a boat on the water?

MORRISON: When you see me here standing and reporting on it.

QUESTION: And you are standing here reporting.

MORRISON: I am not. I am saying there is no such report for me to provide to you today. There is therefore no significant event for me to report at sea.

*

QUESTION: Isn't it significant that just a week or so after you were saying now boats aren't leaving, you haven't had a boat in six months successfully arrive, that we are getting now reports that a boat has come very close to arriving, is in distress. Isn't that a significant shift in what you have been reporting over the past few months?

MORRISON: No.

QUESTION: It seems to be, there is a boat arriving and . . .

MORRISON: Well, a boat hasn't arrived, let's be clear about that and secondly . . .

QUESTION: Can we just decode this, are you saying there is no evidence of there being a boat . . .

MORRISON: I am simply following the same practice, Mark, that I have followed for the last nine months since being in this job. Now, I don't know why anyone would think the government would be departing from our policies and practices in this area. That should come as no surprise to you. The government is doing what we said we would do. The policies are being employed as we said they would be employed and the results we are getting are the results that we said we would get. Now there are many, I suspect even some with me here today who thought that that would not be possible, that it could not be done. But it has been done to date and it will continue to be done to date and going forward and we will continue to apply the policies as we have. That is the government's position. The people smugglers know it, the Australian people know it and that is why they trust us to protect the borders.

QUESTION: Minister, you just said a boat hasn't arrived, that means Australian waters does it?

MORRISON: I said what I said. So you can take it as I said it.

QUESTION: Well, could you just clarify what you meant by that comment?

MORRISON: No, you can read back the transcript. It is fairly clear.

QUESTION: I can remember what you said.

MORRISON: Well, there you go, you don't need that clarified any further.

———

Morrison's habit of withholding anything that might be construed as having a clear and definite meaning was apparent well before his immigration role. In his late twenties, working in tourism, he had been asked about the closing ceremony for the 1996 Atlanta Olympic Games, and the parts representing Sydney, the next host city. *The Sydney Morning Herald* reported: 'Asked about the giant kangaroos on bicycles, Mr Morrison paused before responding. "Kangaroos, they are always popular," he finally said.'

A few years later, Morrison had moved to New Zealand and become a public servant, still in the area of tourism. In 1999, the first profile of him was published. He refused to give his precise age:

> Hunkered behind his desk with a coffee mug clutched in two hands, he looks like almost any other bureaucrat confronted by a reporter armed with a tape recorder and a notebook – nervous. A former front-row forward, he is solidly built, has short brown hair, wears metal-frame glasses and looks young. How young, he will not say, owning only to being 'in my 30s'.

Morrison was thirty, and obviously wanted to be thought of as older than he was.

By 2003, he was in another bureaucratic, backroom role, as the New South Wales Liberal Party's state director. During that year's state election, Lisa Carty, of the *Illawarra Mercury*, called to ask him about a poster intended to promote the Liberal candidate for the district of Keira. The poster, Carty informed him, had the 'i' and the 'e' in the wrong places. Morrison 'greeted the news with stunned silence', wrote Carty. 'After several seconds, when prompted to speak, he said: "I am not about to say anything. I am not saying anything on the record." Clearly, he was not speaking off the record either, because he lapsed into another silence.' Finally, Morrison told Carty he'd call her back.

———

Not answering questions is a way of ensuring there is no record against which your later words or behaviour can be checked. But there is another technique that yields equivalent results, which is simply to deny the record that is there.

In 2012, Jane Cadzow asked Morrison about accusations of scaremongering on immigration. She brought up comments he had made about asylum seekers being sick with diseases such as typhoid. Morrison gave a definitive answer: 'I simply said that people turned up who had these conditions . . . I made no statement about the broader impact or risk.' But, Cadzow pointed out, this was untrue: he had explicitly warned of the risk that these diseases would spread to the mainland.

In 2014, Greens senator Sarah Hanson-Young wrote to Morrison with allegations that underage asylum seekers on Nauru had been forced to have sex in front of a guard. There were also allegations that women were being told to strip in exchange for showers of longer than two minutes. A few days later Morrison announced an independent inquiry. This seems like a reasonable response – but there was a twist. The review would also look into accusations that the allegations had been concocted. Ten staff from Save the Children – an organisation which attempts to do exactly what its name suggests – would be removed from Nauru. They were 'employed to do a job, not to be political activists', said Morrison. 'Making false claims, and worse allegedly coaching self-harm and using children in protests, is unacceptable.'

Morrison had smeared well-meaning staff – men and women who were trying to help children. After the review, the department admitted the staff should not have been removed. It declared there had been 'no reason to cause doubt to be cast' on Save the Children's reputation, and paid the affected staff compensation.

When ABC journalist Barrie Cassidy asked Morrison – now treasurer, with the immigration portfolio behind him – about this damning reversal, he was as definitive as he had been about typhoid: 'I drew no conclusions on the material that had been presented to me at the time.'

Cassidy, in response, was just as clear: 'Well, yes, you did.'

Morrison said, 'No, I didn't, Barrie,' and told Cassidy to go back and check the transcript.

Cassidy said, 'I have.'

Morrison's final line of defence was this: 'I did the job that I had to do in that situation, just as I am doing the job now as treasurer.'

This is similar to what Morrison had said to Crabb – that he had only done the job Tony Abbott had asked him to do. Anything done in that job was reflective of the role itself, and not of the man occupying that role. Perhaps this explains his insistence that he had not said things he clearly had: it was the immigration minister who had said such things, not Scott Morrison himself.

———

If there was an exception to Morrison's unwillingness to stick to a position, you might expect to discover it through his religious beliefs. It would be hard to overstate the role of religion in Morrison's life. He recently told the journalist Greg Sheridan that he reads the Bible frequently: 'It's got easier now that it's on your mobile phone.' He said, too, that he tries to pray every day: 'When I can I'll get down on my knees. Getting down on your knees is a sign of complete dependence in your life. Other prayer is conversational, in the garden at home or wherever.'

Morrison's commitment to God began early. He recounted the decisive moment to Sheridan – he was at a Boys' Brigade camp in Melbourne: 'On that camp I gave my life to the Lord, on January 11, 1981. I was 12. I massively felt it that day . . . It is a confession of repentance. I felt that movement, to get to my feet. I spent the rest of the day sitting with the chaplain.' This was no passing childhood passion: as a young man, Morrison wanted to study theology in Canada, but he had married not long before, and his father secretly arranged a job offer that Morrison then accepted. Today, he attends church regularly and has personal relationships with his pastors; as he told Sheridan, he 'couldn't function' without his faith.

There are few things more telling about a soul than the answers it gives to fundamental questions about the universe. This is Morrison's contention too. In his maiden speech to parliament, Morrison said that his faith was one of the two greatest influences on his life, along with family. The speech is often quoted in part, but you cannot get a proper sense of it without reading this passage in full:

For me, faith is personal, but the implications are social – as personal and social responsibility are at the heart of the Christian message. In recent times it has become fashionable to negatively stereotype those who profess their Christian faith in public life as 'extreme' and to suggest that such faith has no place in the political debate of this country. This presents a significant challenge for those of us, like my colleague, who seek to follow the example of William Wilberforce or Desmond Tutu, to name just two. These leaders stood for the immutable truths and principles of the Christian faith. They transformed their nations and, indeed, the world in the process. More importantly, by following the convictions of their faith, they established and reinforced the principles of our liberal democracy upon which our own nation is built.

Australia is not a secular country – it is a free country. This is a nation where you have the freedom to follow any belief system you choose. Secularism is just one. It has no greater claim than any other on our society. As US Senator Joe Lieberman said, the Constitution guarantees freedom of religion, not from religion. I believe the same is true in this country.

So what values do I derive from my faith? My answer comes from Jeremiah, chapter 9:24: *I am the Lord who exercises loving-kindness, justice and righteousness on earth; for I delight in these things, declares the Lord.*

From my faith I derive the values of loving-kindness, justice and righteousness, to act with compassion and kindness, acknowledging our common humanity and to consider the welfare of others; to fight for a fair go for everyone to fulfil their human potential and to remove whatever unjust obstacles stand in their way, including diminishing their personal responsibility for their own wellbeing; and to do what is right, to respect the rule of law, the sanctity of human life and the moral integrity of marriage and the family. We must recognise an unchanging and absolute standard of what is good and what is evil. Desmond Tutu put it this way: 'we expect Christians . . . to be those who stand up for the truth, to stand up for justice, to stand on the side of the poor and the hungry, the homeless and the naked, and when that happens, then Christians will be trustworthy believable witnesses'.

These are my principles.

The significance of these principles is not limited to Morrison's private life. In the speech, he insists that his personal faith should have repercussions beyond himself. He begins by saying that his faith is personal, but in the same breath says 'the implications are social'. If this phrase seems ambiguous, the next section makes its meaning clear: he holds himself out as somebody who follows Wilberforce and Tutu – men who, he says, 'transformed their nations and, indeed, the world' by standing for 'the immutable truths and principles of the Christian faith'. This, then, is what Morrison has said he wants for himself: to change his nation by following the principles of his faith.

Morrison refused to be held to these words. Four years later, journalist Julia Baird asked him what it meant to be a politician who was also Christian. Morrison said it informed his worldview, but 'the Bible is not a policy handbook. And I get very worried when

people try to treat it like one.' Three years after that, when Jane
Cadzow asked how his faith fitted with his treatment of asylum
seekers, he told her: 'How I reconcile that with my faith is, frankly,
a matter for me.'

That would be true if he had not spoken about his faith as a
guide to his intentions, in very specific terms. He was not being
asked to do something special because he was religious. He was
merely being asked to do what every politician is asked to do: reconcile his actions with his public speech. Religion offered him a
neat trick: a way to articulate values, to make it clear he had them,
while forcefully pushing back on any suggestion that he should be
held to them; even to bring up the question was to risk the suggestion you had somehow breached etiquette.

If the question of whether Morrison has since, in his own
mind, broken with his principles remains impenetrable, the facts
offer a more objective view. Most maiden speeches assert values
without proposing specific policies, and Morrison's was no different – with one exception. Having quoted Desmond Tutu on the
responsibility of Christians 'to stand on the side of the poor and
the hungry, the homeless and the naked', Morrison spoke about
foreign aid in emotive terms: 'Our attention in this area cannot
be limited only to areas of strategic self-interest. It must be pursued as the responsibility of our common humanity. In Africa,
6500 people die every day from preventable and treatable diseases. Africa . . . is a true moral crisis that eclipses all others.' The
government had already increased aid, he said – now it must go
further. 'The need is not diminishing, nor can our support. It is
the Australian thing to do.'

Eight years later, Morrison delivered his first budget as treasurer of Australia. He cut foreign aid by $200 million. He said that it was Labor's fault for blowing the surplus.

In 2021, facing more scrutiny than ever before, Morrison departed completely – at least publicly – from his earlier proclamations about transforming the nation and the world through devotion to Christian values. His faith, he told Sheridan, has 'got nothing to do with politics'.

Once again, our gaze finds nothing on which it can fix.

———

Morrison's father, John, who grew up in the Presbyterian faith, was a committed Christian, which Morrison has said is one of several legacies his father left him. Morrison was closely involved with church groups through his childhood – that was how he met Jenny.

Later, he began attending evangelical churches. His attachment to Pentecostal Christianity has attracted comment because of some of that church's more unusual beliefs, like the ability of certain believers to speak in tongues (Morrison does not do so). Many Australians would be unfamiliar with the showbiz style of some evangelical churches. Here is journalist Jacqueline Maley's description of her visit to the church Morrison attends:

[We enter] the church's auditorium, which can hold up to 1000 worshippers. It is dark, with coloured concert lighting and stage smoke. A large curved stage takes the place of an altar, and there is none of the usual Christian iconography you would expect in a church. Behind the stage is an enormous screen that lights up over the next hour and a half, with the lyrics of the Christian contemporary songs performed by the five-piece band, advertisements for Horizon Church activities and programs, and prompts about the various ways you can give the church money. A card placed on our seats also lists 'giving options' . . .

Sound technicians in headphones check levels from a podium in the bleachers. On stage, the band plays, and a troupe of five 20-somethings sings about Jesus. The atmosphere feels wholesome and upbeat, like an audition round for *Australian Idol*. Everyone in tonight's 300-strong congregation is super-excited to be here, and already a throng of young worshippers crowds the stage, swaying and clapping to the music, their faces upturned to the singers.

In a long analysis of Morrison's religious beliefs, the historian James Boyce points out that Pentecostalism is less reliant on dogma than other branches of Christianity. He writes: 'The essence of our prime minister's religion is not a set of beliefs at all but a unique perspective on the Christian experience in which God is so intimately present to the saved and sanctified that he can be felt, talked to and heard at any time.'

In fact, writes Boyce, a shifting set of specific convictions might even be justified by a strong evangelical faith. 'Mutability co-exists with conviction because the conviction is genuine: Jesus is always in charge. Policy changes and loyalty realignments can be proclaimed with self-righteous certainty because the proclaimer knows that Christ is always present.'

———

Most of us are reasonably free to tell the story of our lives without hindrance. Our greatest obstacle might be that we are rarely asked to tell it. But on the occasions that we are, we can more or less weave whatever tale we choose; we can omit, and include, at will; we can rewrite how we felt about things at the time; we can lie about how we feel about them now. Even if we can persuade the person listening to show an interest – or even to be genuinely interested – they are unlikely to interrogate what we are saying, and certainly not publicly. If we are not entirely the authors of our own lives, we are at least the authors of the stories told about our lives.

But politicians – or, more broadly, celebrities, of whom politicians are one unglamorous subset – require assistance in presenting their story. This is for the simple reason that they must get that story out to as many people as possible. They need journalists to join their cause. If a politician is, for most of us, no more than a character in a book, then political journalists, taken as a group, are the authors of that book.

Much has been written about the unequal relationship between journalists and their subjects. The most famous statement of the problem comes from Janet Malcolm – the writer who told the psychiatrist he was treating the murderer as a character in a book – who, across her career, spent many thousands of words examining the struggle between those written about and those writing. Inevitably, she argued, the journalist lures her subject into a web of delusion, in which the subject believes he will succeed in convincing the journalist to tell his story. But the journalist only ever wants to tell *her* story; and, finally, because she holds the pen, that is what she does.

This is summarised in the opening to Malcolm's work *The Journalist and the Murderer*, published in 1990: 'Every journalist who is not too stupid or too full of himself to notice what is going on knows that what he does is morally indefensible. He is a kind of confidence man, preying on people's vanity, ignorance or loneliness, gaining their trust and betraying them without remorse.' At the time, this was attacked as an unfair generalisation. Malcolm would later tell *The Paris Review*:

> When I wrote *The Journalist and the Murderer*, I guess I was (not all that subtly) separating myself from the herd of journalists, and a lot of them got mad at me for breaking ranks. There was something deeply irritating about this woman who set herself up as being more honest and clear-sighted than anyone else. My analysis of journalistic betrayal was seen as a betrayal of journalism itself as well as a piece of royal chutzpah. Today, my critique seems obvious, even banal.

She is right – few journalists would, today, quibble with the description. But the interaction between the press and politicians is not quite as she describes. Politicians possess an almost unique awareness of the rules of the journalistic game. More importantly, they also possess a power that most subjects do not: the journalist writing about them makes her living from writing about the same people, over and over and over again. Inevitably, she will, at some point, hope that this politician favours her with access and leaked stories. At the very least, she will not want to foreclose that possibility forever by being nasty to that politician.

Some journalists succeed in resisting the pressure this creates. But the overwhelming majority do not, and they create a centre of gravity for the others. By treating a politician very gently on many occasions – what they would call 'even-handedly' – they make it harder for other journalists to stray too far from these gentle verdicts, lest they look sharply partisan by comparison. It is not surprising that Cadzow, whose profile remains among the most damning and incisive pieces of writing about Morrison, is not dependent on writing about politics for her livelihood, but writes profiles on a range of people. Preserving the good opinions of Morrison, his political party or political writers was not, for her, a matter of professional importance.

The word 'pragmatic' became one such centre of gravity. It is often used, now, by Morrison's critics as much as by his fans. This is telling, because there are many other ways that Morrison's willingness to switch positions or abandon values he once proclaimed might have been presented. He could have been called 'ruthless' or 'cunning'. He might have been 'a moral vacuum', or 'amoral', or perhaps 'vacuous'. He could have been branded 'delusional', given he seemed to believe he had not said things he had. Or perhaps his switching back and forth, depending on what voters seemed to want, could have been 'weak'. 'Pragmatic' is the word that said least, and was therefore sufficiently neutral to carry a spectrum of meanings. But that does not mean it was the closest to the truth.

SUBURBAN

Observing how determined Scott Morrison's performance has been could lead easily to cynicism and the assumption that all of this is made up. Such logic leads nowhere. If the image Morrison constantly seeks to portray is false, this implies there must be some true Morrison he has hidden from us, lurking out of sight. Across so long a period in public life, one would expect this alternative persona to slip out at some point – but this is, to a very large extent, not the case. When other facts – such as his brief love affair with Australian Rules – emerge to cast doubt on the specifics of the picture Morrison has painted, there is no obvious *real* Morrison they point us to, one possessing a different sensibility, another way of being in the world.

And yet it is hard to feel that there is not something odd about this diligently achieved picture. It is too perfectly calibrated, too perfectly representative of a certain version of Australianness – as though the man himself had been created out of the desires of a focus group. We know, too, that Morrison understood this representation would work to his advantage, from the time and effort he put into making sure we knew all about it.

In his classic account of Australian society, *The Lucky Country*, Donald Horne writes that sport 'to many Australians is life and the rest a shadow'. It was also a proxy for our relationship to the nation. 'To play sport, or watch others play, and to read and talk about it was to uphold the nation and build its character.' By placing his love of sport at the centre of his public persona, Morrison was billing himself as essentially Australian and also as somebody who loved what it was to be Australian. Rugby league added a class-based appeal to this image.

The adoption of a specific team was important. John Howard liked rugby league, and rather quietly supported the St. George Illawarra Dragons; but this was not the team from the area he represented. Morrison supported the club which represented the suburban community in which he lived, the Sutherland Shire – which he mentioned almost as often as the Sharks.

Elsewhere in *The Lucky Country*, Horne described Australia as 'the first suburban nation'. When he wrote this, Australia's status as suburban was, by Horne's account, not yet entirely accepted. This was in part because the nation still clung to an idea of itself as a 'race of laconic country folk'. The idea of suburbs carried a sense of affluence that ran against the notion of being working-class, which was the other part of the nation's identity. As well, elites, who controlled much of the public image of Australia, hated the idea of suburbs, and tended to ignore them.

By now, Australia has embraced its affluence. Living in the suburbs has become a way to define yourself against both poverty and snobbish elites. Morrison's constant references to the Sharks and the Shire ensured that this positioning was communicated to as many people as possible. In this repetition was something else, too: a sense of defiant pride in this identity.

As with rugby league, the picture of this Shire devotee was not precisely accurate. Morrison's love for the Shire seems sincere. Still, he grew up in Bronte, in Sydney's Eastern Suburbs. In 2016, he talked about his attachment to the Shire: 'Bronte wouldn't feel like home to me today.' That may be true, but he was not talking about a distant memory: he and Jenny bought a bungalow in Bronte in 1995, and only sold it in 2009.

In an email to constituents after he became prime minister, Morrison wrote: 'Our house in the shire is a typical family home. It has a mortgage, it needs a bit of work and no front fence.' In an interview with *The Daily Telegraph* around the same time, he was more specific: 'My mortgage is about the average size, it isn't a zero, it's still got lots of zeroes on it and we'll deal with that like any other family.' Again, this is likely true, but at the time the Morrisons bought the house, for $920,000, that was nearly twice the median house price in the area. One expert publicly suggested it would be worth double that now. Morrison is not extremely rich, but he is still far richer than most: this is a man who has earned between $100,000 and $300,000 per year for most of his working life.

———

Morrison might not have grown up in the Shire, but he did have a suburban childhood. When Morrison was a child, his parents ran a local theatre group. One year, the whole family appeared in the local production of *Oliver!*. Mr Morrison played Fagin, and Scott played a skilled young pickpocket, the Artful Dodger.

After this, Morrison's mother decided Scott had what it took. Arrangements were made with an agent, and the boy took part in photo shoots, acted in TV ads. At some point he got out of the business – but it had not left him with nothing.

Morrison's first job was with the Property Council of Australia, which lobbies governments on behalf of developers. One day he came up with an idea and left the office to buy a set of scales. The man who hired him was later quoted in *The Australian Financial Review*:

> Scott displayed a unique capacity to communicate ideas in a persuasive and telling manner. It was his idea to spotlight the duplication of Australia's planning regimes by weighing them all . . . The pile of laws weighed-in at 28 kilos and triggered fruitful discussions about solutions that would serve the broader community.

Morrison had left advertising and found a way to go back into advertising.

From there he moved to another lobbying job, in a different industry. Morrison has held four jobs in tourism – a field that is also largely about advertising – and has exited each under a cloud. He left the first to work for his organisation's direct competitor. His new organisation went bankrupt, which some blamed partly on his management.

At that point he left Australia. Soon after, working for the New Zealand government, he pushed for several senior figures to quit. They did, and the affair became a mess. Within a year, the minister for whom Morrison had worked was sacked. It became a political crisis for the prime minister, Jenny Shipley. New Zealand newspaper *The Dominion* described it as a 'fiasco', and Morrison as 'a cross between Rasputin and Crocodile Dundee'.

Morrison moved back to Australia and worked briefly for consultants KPMG, where it seems he attempted to establish a tourism section. That didn't work out, and he went to work for the Liberal Party. Then, in 2005, he was appointed head of Tourism Australia.

That job, too, ended early. There had been tensions with the minister, Fran Bailey. Morrison thought he would have the prime minister, John Howard – for whom he had worked on the 2004 federal election campaign – on his side. Howard, though, always backed his ministers, and Morrison was sacked by the board. Morrison had been paid $300,000 a year to do the job; he was reportedly paid more to leave.

———

Before he left, Morrison's main task had been to lead the effort to come up with a new tourism campaign for the nation. The ad that resulted was tested with 47,000 people in eighty-six focus groups across seven countries. It cost $180 million – about what it cost to make a big-budget Hollywood film – and resulted in a series of Australian cliches. Here is my summary:

'We've bought you a beer,' says a man in an Akubra drinking a beer in a pub.

'And we've had the camel shampooed,' says a woman in the desert, leading camels.

'We've saved you a spot on the beach,' says a young woman in a bikini walking out of the ocean (while a didgeridoo starts playing in the background).

'And we've got the sharks out of the pool,' says a young boy in an ocean pool.

'We got the roos off the green,' says a middle-aged man on a golf course, kangaroos watching on.

'And Bill's on his way down to open the front gate,' says a man in an Akubra-like hat, on the porch of a farmhouse.

'Your taxi's waiting,' says a seaplane pilot.

'And dinner's about to be served,' says a waiter in front of Uluru.

'We've turned on the lights,' says a young woman in front of Harbour Bridge fireworks.

'And we've been rehearsing for over 40,000 years,' says an Indigenous woman with other Indigenous people in face paint, dancing in the desert.

'So where the bloody hell are you?' asks the bikinied woman, still on the beach.

John Howard had complained a month earlier of 'the increasing use of vulgarism' on television. 'Earthiness of expression in an appropriate environment is something to be encouraged, but the use of vulgar language is not necessarily something that makes us a better, more expressive people,' he said. Now, Howard was asked to defend the use of 'bloody', and did so:

> I think it is a colloquialism, it's not a word that is seen quite
> in the same category as other words that nobody ought to use
> in public or on the media or in advertisements . . . I think the
> style of the advertisement is anything but offensive, it is in
> fact in context and I think it's a very effective ad . . . I think

watching that young girl walking up the beach, I don't think there's anything bad-mannered about that.

The ad was banned on UK television for use of the word. The Australian media loved the story, and there were suggestions that Morrison had planned it all along, which he denied. But, as is often the case with foreign interest in Australia, more was made of the matter locally than seemed justified by the level of attention overseas. A more sober report in *The Sydney Morning Herald* (written in part by Annabel Crabb) stated: 'News of the banning was carried in some British newspapers, but received only minor treatment.' The ban was lifted less than two weeks after it was imposed.

It is unclear whether the ad did what it was supposed to. Tourism revenue rose, partly because tourists came for longer, but the actual number of tourists remained flat. In 2008, when the campaign was cancelled, Morrison defended it at length in parliament, saying the aim had been to increase spending, not the number of tourists. But when Morrison was appointed to the role, the chair of the agency had expressed the hope that he would increase both spending and visitors, and Morrison himself had said the same.

The 'Where the bloody hell are you?' ad trades in stereotypes we are unlikely to see again. Today, it appears dated; it is too simple, too daggy, for our knowing times. And yet it is obviously a good ad. It makes you feel good, the pictures are attractive, the tune is catchy, it pulls you along with its momentum.

This effectiveness is very deliberately achieved. Unlike many ads, there is no attempt to tell a story: instead, there is a series of crisp images. The viewer is not told, in didactic fashion, about the attractions on offer; they are shown instead. Finally, it leans heavily on the idea of a uniquely Australian identity. What is communicated to the viewer is not so much any specific information as a particular aura, built around the idea of the stereotypical Australian. Here is Morrison describing the ad in roughly the same terms he will later use to describe the strategy a politician needs to sell himself:

> Unless we were authentic, unless we were fair dinkum, unless we were real, they [the target markets] would reject any message we put forward. Hence, we've come up with something which is very authentic, very real and uniquely Australian in terms of how we try to put this campaign together.

Morrison also offered a more granular view of what was needed in effective advertising campaigns. In an interview with *Marketing* magazine just after the campaign had been launched, he said: 'Tourism Australia runs both small and large-scale promotions. What is consistent across both, however, is the messaging – whether it be a radio promotion in Germany or a print promotion in the US, the messaging will be consistent with the advertising and PR campaign.'

———

Acting together as part of the theatre group was one way the Morrisons spent time together, Morrison told Crabb on *Kitchen Cabinet*; otherwise, they were too busy. In part, this was because of his father's involvement in local politics. John Morrison was a policeman and a councillor and eventually a mayor. Young Scott would help out with the politics, answering phone calls from constituents and going around the local area with his father, knocking on doors, hoping for the chance to be invited in and convince the householder to vote the right way. Scott liked the doorknocking, he told Crabb, because 'I quite enjoyed the theatre of it all'.

Theatrical metaphors crop up at crucial moments in Morrison's career. The 'Muppet Show' reference became briefly notorious, but what is more interesting, at this distance, is the theatrical echo of the words that Morrison chose: 'The curtain's come down . . . and an absolute new curtain has lifted up.'

Most interesting is that 2017 interview with Sharri Markson, which seems to have defined so much of what came after. Morrison told Markson that voters were no longer attracted to 'the staged nature of politics'. But then, in the speech delivered in conjunction with the interview, Morrison also chose a theatrical metaphor, this time to explain what voters wanted instead: politicians who 'took on the role of the authentic outsider'.

Morrison was not suggesting that voters wanted *actual* outsiders, nor that his party should seek them out and promote them. He was not suggesting substantive or structural change of any sort. Instead, he was telling his colleagues that this was a matter of performance, of the *roles* politicians *took on*. The word 'role' was probably used lazily, but it is telling, because as a political insider himself, performing that role was the only option open to Morrison. He would never be an actual outsider, but he could play the part.

The metaphors that people use are often revealing. After I left politics, I noticed a widespread tendency among former staffers to speak of PTSD, or post-traumatic stress disorder – a form of suffering more often experienced by soldiers or survivors of violent assault. This was obviously an exaggeration. The exaggeration was part of the point: by ostentatiously playing up the extent of their wound, the staffers – white-collar workers who faced few real threats – were undercutting their own complaint, making it clear that they did not take themselves as seriously as all that. Having made this clear, they were able to point to the real pain beneath, the one they felt not quite able to talk about – the pain that came from long hours, constant pressure, insane bosses and intense public scrutiny. There was something about the metaphor that was true and something that was untrue, and both elements were needed to convey an accurate impression.

This is how all metaphors work: they communicate meaning in two ways, from their similarity to the object being described and their difference from it. It is these two aspects, together, that enable us to see the object being described more clearly.

One could derive from these theatrical metaphors the idea that Morrison is dishonest, an actor seeking to give a false impression. This conclusion is too easy. Morrison's political behaviour bears a similarity to theatre and also a difference. The similarity is that Morrison is constantly performing. But in theatre, what you perform is made up. Morrison is performing something that is, in its essence, true. This is the difference.

When Morrison said he wanted to leave 'the staged nature of politics' behind, in order to take on 'the role of the authentic outsider', it was clear, from his language, that he was not seeking to leave performance behind altogether. What he believed voters disliked was the *feeling* that politics was staged. It was this that

politicians needed to move beyond. They should do this – Morrison
would do this – not by abandoning performance, but by turning in
a better performance, of a different kind: by performing himself.

Much of this performance is conscious: the emphasis, the repetition. But the effectiveness of the performance, its convincing
nature, suggests that sometimes Morrison forgets that he is acting.
Someone who has known Morrison since his early career told me,
of the suburban image, 'That is Scott. He's suburban. He's proudly
suburban . . . Aggressively suburban.' But he also said that when
Morrison adopts a stance, 'he makes himself genuinely believe it . . .
Because he can seemingly convince himself of things aggressively.'

———

While writing this book, I discovered the work of T.M. Luhrmann.
An anthropologist, Luhrmann spent several years with evangelical
congregations on the east coast of America. She prayed regularly,
and while, at the conclusion, she did not call herself a Christian, she
found herself defending Christianity. At the centre of Luhrmann's
work is an understanding of how difficult it is to maintain belief in
this century:

Faith asks people to consider that the evidence of their senses
is wrong. In various ways, and in varying degrees, faith asks
that people believe that their minds are not always private;
that persons are not always visible; that invisible presences
should alter their emotions and direct their behavior; that
reality is good and justice triumphant. These are fantastic
claims, and the fact of their improbability is not lost on those

who accept them – particularly in a pluralistic, self-aware society like twenty-first-century America. Many Christians come to their religious commitments slowly, carefully, and deliberatively, as if the attitude they take toward life itself depends upon their judgment. And they doubt. They find it hard to believe in an invisible being – let alone an invisible being who is entirely good and overwhelmingly powerful. Many Christians struggle, at one point or another, with the despair that it all might be a sham.

The evangelical churches in which Luhrmann spent time managed this in various ways, but one way was to invite their congregants to act *as though* God is real; in fact, to act *as though* God is a very good, entirely real friend, someone you might eat a meal with. They were encouraged to *play*, because if you played seriously enough, the play would become reality. Which was, Luhrmann writes, exactly what happened.

When a child plays, they hold two frames in their head at once. In the example Luhrmann gives, the child knows that the water in which she is bathing her teddy bear is not really there. When she dries teddy with her invisible towel, she knows the towel is not there. But she also entirely believes the water and the towel are there, that the teddy is really wet, then really dry. She lives 'on two levels' – just as people of faith live on two levels. Belief involves holding, always, two frames in your head: a *faith frame*, in which God is present and interested and involved, and a *reality frame*, in which the cars around you are moving, the dog needs to be fed, the dishes need to be washed.

Luhrmann is not the first anthropologist to note the overlap between religious belief and play. But, she writes, evangelical practice accentuates the overlap. A God who is intimately involved in your life, who acts almost as a friend, who is interested in what you wear or have for breakfast, who is 'so real, so accessible, and so present', means that these two frames are always operating. You are always in a state of acting *as though* a being you cannot see is real and present.

When I read this, I felt a jolt. What Luhrmann was describing bears such strong similarity to so much of Morrison's behaviour. It seems improbable that Morrison might say so many things that are obviously untrue – that he has not said or done things he has obviously said and done. It seems odd, at least, that he can so determinedly hold himself out as defined by curries and rugby league, quite recent adoptions.

As I read Luhrmann, the pieces settled into place. Morrison knew – from practice, from habit, perhaps not consciously but somewhere deep within – that it was possible to convince yourself of something simply by acting as though it were true. If acting had provided one model for this, religion had provided by far the more important. If you throw yourself into a performance, then you can, at least temporarily, come to believe that the performance is real. This does not require delusion. You know that you have said something; but, at the same time, you believe that you never said such a thing. There are two frames, and you are capable of existing in both at once: the frame in which the world is as you say it is, because you are the prime minister, and the frame in which facts dominate. Morrison's particular skill is to toggle back and forth between these frames as necessary – to believe whichever needs to be believed.

Most of us instinctively understand such behaviour, because, increasingly, most of us toggle between different frames as well. We all, these days, shift between different realities. This is a point Luhrmann makes: we read novels, watch television, place our headphones over our ears and are absorbed into worlds of our own choosing. And we are capable of accepting that events are both real and not-real at once: that the competitors on 'reality television' are both real and performing; that the people we follow on Twitter are both people and characters they are in the process of creating. We might not be quite as adept at this as Morrison, but we are sufficiently schooled in this way of existing not to judge him too much for the over-the-top performance of Aussie blokiness he puts on. We know that it is both real and not-real, because we are real and not-real too.

————

Some novelists like to talk about their characters as though, in the writing process, they become real people. At some point in the writing of the novel, these writers say, the characters escaped their control. They began to stand on their own two feet, spoke when they felt like it, made their own decisions about where to go next. At that point, the book more or less wrote itself.

This is a fantasy, of course. The novelist always had control. And this is very similar to the fantasy to which most journalists remain attached: that they are at the mercy of the flesh-and-blood characters they are following, merely reporting, dutifully, what those real-life characters say and do.

Morrison understands that this is a myth. But he understands, too, that – like any myth – it has enormous power. In those early anecdotes about his brushes with the media, there is a sense of nervous caution. In two, the journalists note a pause before Morrison speaks. But the pause has not been used to come up with an illuminating answer, some articulate demonstration of knowledge or insight. Instead, it has been used to figure out how to put a stop to this line of inquiry, however harmless it might be.

At some point Morrison must have realised this was a mistake – or at least that it was not sustainable. He had left too large a gap. The only thing filling it was his image as a hard-hearted political warrior on the issue of refugees – it might even have been Cadzow's piece that made him see this. In 2015, with the chance of becoming prime minister looming, with an election due not long after that, it was essential for Morrison to fill that gap in some other way. That is when the ScoMo character was first imagined. In 2018, with the same combination of circumstances approaching, he faced much the same challenge, but with three years' readiness behind him. The strategy fell into place.

Morrison's sudden enthusiasm for media appearances, his over-eager desire to talk about himself, is not the opposite of his earlier reluctance to answer questions. It is a more sophisticated version of the same understanding of the world: one in which journalists will, ultimately, be the ones to tell his story. At first, Morrison was able to prevent certain stories from being told, and minimise the amount of attention he received. Later, as his fame grew, he came to understand that, given the inevitability that stories about him would be told, his best option was to play a role in shaping them. And he understood, too, that many journalists felt obliged to report what was put in front of them – if he simply said the word 'pragmatic' often enough, set up the idea of 'authenticity' and spoke about football at every opportunity, then this was the version of him that would reach the public.

The existence of Cadzow's 2012 profile, written before Morrison began his determined 2015 campaign to reinvent himself, is a stroke of luck. It acts as a kind of scientific control, a test against which the later, cloying coverage of Morrison's daggy dad status can be measured. There was nothing inevitable about the way that Morrison was presented to the public just a few years later. The ScoMo character was not the only possible version of Scott Morrison – there was the man who didn't want money spent on relatives attending funerals, or the man with an intense commitment to evangelical Christianity, or the man who couldn't decide which footy team he liked, or the man who fluently lied about what he had and had not said. That 'ScoMo' was the version that came to dominate was not an accident.

———

Morrison's skill in constructing this version of himself should be recognised. First, he adopted his trademark characteristics. Second, he telegraphed them to the public, again and again and again. Third, he convinced journalists to transmit the facts he wanted them to transmit. This last achievement is, especially for a certain type of politician, easier than it sounds. Anyone who works in politics long enough learns that many journalists, like many people in any profession, are short on time. A press secretary writing a press release learns to put the most important information in the first paragraph, the next most important in the next paragraph, and so on, because that is the way the journalists will write their articles, and it pays to make their job easier. Morrison did not simply like rugby league and cook once a week. He covered himself with Sharks paraphernalia, mentioned the team often and found new ways to bring up curry in interviews. He made it easy for journalists to do what he wanted them to do.

None of this would matter if it were not for two other facts. The first is Morrison's understanding – though he would not put it this way – that the journalists he depends on to tell his story are not only like novelists; they are like poor novelists, constantly creating flat characters. In somewhere between 800 and 1500 words, the journalist must present a picture of a politician that the reader will find sufficiently entertaining and, most important, easy to digest. Her aim is to make him recognisable; his aim, provided the portrait is sufficiently flattering, is to be recognisable. Almost inevitably, this means regurgitating the most obvious facets of a politician's life. In Morrison's case, he chose what would be obvious, and journalists went along with it. Their interests coincided.

Much is made of the 'insider' status of reporters, their access to politicians. In Australia we even have a political television show called *Insiders*. This mythology can give the impression that journalists know politicians in ways that voters don't – a point Crabb made in her justification of her show. This is not really true. Politicians are like characters in a novel to the journalists who write about them, too. The journalists will have some personal impressions: perhaps they ate with the politician once, or interviewed them; certainly they will have watched the politician up close at press conferences. But the politicians are performing for the journalists – and the depictions of them the rushed journalists provide to the public are shaped, to a very large extent, by what other people have already written about them, by the widely accepted stories about who they are. Once an impression has been noted down on paper – 'pragmatic', 'authentic' – it will find its way into other reports, and from there it will make its way further.

Still, the credit does not belong entirely to Morrison, nor to the journalists who spread his messages. If journalists are poor novelists, then Crabb, in presenting *Kitchen Cabinet*, takes on the role of a literary novelist, one presenting us with depths, should we wish to notice them. Most of the time, though, we don't – which is why most journalists don't bother. And this is because they recognise, on some level, what Morrison knows in his bones: when it comes to politicians, flat characters – simple, without nuance and easily digestible – are exactly what we, the voters, want.

SLEEPING SOUNDLY

In late September 2018, during the needles-in-strawberries crisis, one of the hosts of *The Today Show*, Karl Stefanovic, concluded an interview with Scott Morrison by asking how long it had been since he'd eaten a strawberry. The prime minister said he'd had one the day before, he was having some with his breakfast that morning, and on the weekend Jen would make a pav and he would make a curry. 'You're putting strawberries in a curry?' joked Karl. 'I mean, that's disgusting.'

Just before this, Karl had put another question to Morrison; it also sounded a little like a joke. 'Do you really have a trophy in your office saying "I stopped the boats"?'

The existence of the trophy had been discovered by two journalists from *The New York Times*, columnist Maureen Dowd and the Australian bureau chief, Damien Cave. Cave noted that it was not the only celebration of Morrison's time in immigration on display: there was also a Border Force baseball cap and a glass trophy from a ceremony for a naval vessel. But it was the small trophy cut from shiny metal which attracted attention. There was a black line, indicating waves, at its base, and an unfussy black sans-serif font running across it, reading 'I Stopped These'. It was shaped like the boats which typically carried refugees – it could easily have been the boat that crashed into Christmas Island.

Morrison has always been reticent about his feelings. As immigration minister, he was asked how he felt when asylum seekers died at sea or were beaten to death in one of the camps for which he was responsible. 'I know what I think, I know how I respond and I largely consider those things more personal, how I process them . . . People aren't looking for me, frankly, to conduct myself as if I'm sitting on Oprah's couch.'

He has also made it known that he is affected by these events – that he has felt terrible sadness:

You must confront the terrible realities of these things . . .
You don't become immune to them, you never do. And nor
should you. You must maintain a vulnerability to the human
consequences of all of this. Now whether that comes across
in how I present, that's for others to judge.

It has been reported that Morrison wept at the news of the Christmas Island tragedy. He has talked of the 'moral burdens' attached to the decisions he has had to take.

This is why the trophy struck so many as graceless: where were the moral burdens?

In answer to Stefanovic's question – 'Do you really have a trophy in your office saying "I stopped the boats"?' – Morrison replied, 'Yeah, no one in the Labor Party has one like that, I can tell you, because they didn't.'

———

The trophy is not only graceless: it is also odd. The gaps or contradictions in the way that Morrison approaches the world should create in us a sense of curiosity, a desire to look closer to find the clue that might make sense of them; in other words, Morrison should intrigue us. Instead, something about the man tends to produce the opposite effect. When I told people I was writing this book, the reaction I encountered most often was pity for the task I was enduring.

I can understand this – when I was first approached by my publisher to write a book about Morrison, perhaps a biography, I said no; I simply could not summon up sufficient interest in the man. Nor am I the only one who has felt this way – here is David Marr, writing in Quarterly Essay correspondence in 2020:

> Pollsters and journalists weren't the only ones caught unawares last May. So were publishers. Nothing on Morrison hit the market before or after his miracle victory. No biographies charting his rise and, it must be said, no Quarterly Essay exploring his character. We didn't bother. It wasn't just that Morrison seemed destined to lose. There was something else, something we mistakenly thought would underwrite his loss: he wasn't interesting.
>
> We knew enough about Morrison the man not to want to know more – the sackings, the happy clapper faith, the ugly scramble through the ranks to snatch preselection, his ambiguous role in the slaughter of Turnbull. But there wasn't much curiosity to know more. So despite the return of the Coalition government there was nothing in the shops from Allen

& Unwin or Scribe or Black Inc. The verdict of the publishing trade was: adios.

Given everything we know about him – the contradictions, the denials, the relentless self-presentation – the fact that we are not interested should, itself, surprise us. We should stop to ask the question: how is it that Morrison repels interest so? It is surely not sufficient to stop at Marr's sharp formula, 'We knew enough about Morrison the man not to want to know more.'

———

One part of the answer might be simple snobbishness – the same snobbishness that means that elites, so called, still despise the suburbs. Morrison's self-presentation as the epitome of traditional Australia means that he also comes across as ordinary – relentlessly so. His musical taste is middle-of-the-road. His interests are unintellectual. His language is banal.

In fact, his language is worse than banal. In his tussles with the media, in so many of his public declarations, there is a common element: they border on the absurd. They are asymptotic to meaning, sidling right up to the edge of being comprehensible, of resembling ordinary human communication, before sliding away again. Whether Morrison is delivering a prepared address or answering questions from journalists on the spot, there is the same calculation, made tangible in that pause before he says almost nothing: the considered decision to avoid communicating meaning of any sort.

Noticing this could easily lead us into an error: one similar to assuming that Morrison's determined performance means there is some other Morrison we have not yet glimpsed. We could decide that Morrison's words are disconnected from the man; that he keeps his real words, his real thoughts hidden. But just as Morrison's performance is ultimately a performance of himself, his words are likely to be a more concentrated version of the man. They are, after all, carefully chosen. Phrases recur and patterns are evident.

The journalist Katharine Murphy has recounted a story about Morrison when he was treasurer, told to her by independent senator Nick Xenophon:

> Lower house MPs had filed into the Senate chamber for the governor-general's speech, and were in the process of filing out when the milling throng brought Xenophon and Morrison together. Xenophon at the time was an influential player in the Senate, a vote the government needed periodically. 'I said to [Morrison] it would be good to catch up for a coffee, because I actually enjoyed talking to him about policy,' Xenophon recalls. 'He looked at me askance and said, "What for?" I said just to catch up and have a chat about issues. He said, "No, mate. I'm purely transactional."' Xenophon laughs at the memory, but he wasn't laughing at the time. 'It was pretty blunt. It was a pretty terse response, basically fobbing me off. I thought, okay. I felt a bit chastised. I thought this isn't someone you want to shoot the breeze with. "I'm purely transactional." I was taken aback. I thought I had worked pretty constructively with him, even on the asylum seeker issue.'

In this fascinating anecdote, full of Xenophon's injured pride, Morrison appears, on first reading, scrupulously honest. This honesty comes at the cost of the ordinary social niceties most of us take for granted. Xenophon's shock suggests that their earlier interactions – when Morrison had needed him – had given him a very different impression, that the pleasant manner Morrison had displayed might last beyond that specific moment. Most of us, once we have been nice to someone, feel the pull of obligation, the need to be nice to them again, to carry on in the same vein lest the earlier interaction be rendered obviously false in retrospect. Having been, perhaps, insincerely nice, for reasons of convenience or need, we feel we have accrued a debt; that debt can only be paid (perversely enough) by continuing the insincerity. In other words, we act, in each moment, as though it is just one of many moments stretching out before and behind us, and which are connected to each other. Xenophon's tale suggests that for Morrison, each moment stands alone. For him, an interaction demands only what it demands: he will do what needs to be done at that precise point in time. He never feels, in himself, insincere or untruthful, because he always means exactly what he says; it is just that he means it only in the moment he is saying it. Past and future disappear.

This suggests a tantalising possibility. When Morrison sent that queasily pleasant text message to Malcolm Turnbull, right after he had taken the prime ministership, Turnbull likely believed it to be genuine. Later, he came to see it as the insincere act of a hypocrite – certainly, when he included it in his book, that is how he intended us to read it. It is possible, though, that Morrison believed what he said entirely – that whatever had happened in the days before was, in some sense, unavailable to him. When he sent that message, the past no longer existed.

This may explain why it is so difficult to understand Morrison beyond the most basic facts. Most of us make sense of the world through story, which depends on chronology and causation: this happened, and this made that happen, and that caused this other thing to happen. This is how language works as well. Each sentence tells a story – subject, verb, object – something did something to something else.

For Morrison, there is no story; events are not joined. His perception of the world is like that ad for Australia he once helped create: a series of crisp images, each separate from the next. This is the way he speaks, which is very possibly the way he thinks.

And this is how Morrison comes across, isn't it? We see a series of images of the man, never the man himself or a story that might help make sense of him. He is kicking a football; he is cooking a curry; he is wearing an orange hi-vis vest; he is stopping the boats; he is overseeing a regime in which children suffer; he is hugging his family.

———

Perhaps this makes sense of the trophy, too.

Morrison told Jane Cadzow, 'What you have to do in this portfolio is just be very comfortable in your own skin about the decisions you're taking and why you are taking them. And I am.' To Annabel Crabb, he said, 'The thing none of us like about politics is many of the things you've raised today, about what does such-and-such think about this – I've just learnt not to care. And I really don't that much.'

Both Cadzow and Crabb, who had spent some time with Morrison, redescribed this attitude in their own words. Each used expressions involving sleep and the idea that Morrison slept well. Cadzow wrote that he had 'the clear eyes and smooth visage of one who sleeps soundly at night'. After hosting him on *Kitchen Cabinet*, Crabb said, 'He really didn't seem to care at all. I think that is why he is a really powerful figure in the Coalition; he does the awful work that makes people yell at you in the street, and he doesn't lie awake worrying about people hating him.'

When somebody has a guilty conscience, we say that they have troubled dreams. In Shakespeare's greatest tale of guilt, Macbeth, having murdered, loses the ability to sleep – he keeps hearing, instead, an insistent voice: 'Macbeth has murdered sleep, and therefore Macbeth will sleep no more.' He says this to Lady Macbeth, immediately after he has told her something else: that he cannot pray either.

Why can Macbeth neither sleep nor pray? Shakespeare gives the answer: 'My dull brain was wrought / With things forgotten.' It is not that Macbeth is a moral man – he has killed for ambition. Rather, as critic James Wood writes, it is that Macbeth has an active memory, one that will not leave him alone.

In an interview with Katharine Murphy, Morrison told her he had a terrible memory. Instead, he said, 'I have a flow brain.'

This is one of those awful phrases kidnapped from psychology and imported into business schools. In short, it means to be utterly sunk in your work, so immersed that time begins to fly. In a TED

Talk about the flow state, Mihaly Csikszentmihalyi, the psychologist who coined the term, explained what it was like: the task just goes by automatically, he said. 'You don't think.'

I cannot say whether Morrison feels the moral burdens of refugee policy strongly or weakly, deeply or only at a shallow level. I wonder, though, whether these metaphors are a way to search in the wrong place: perhaps he feels things both deeply and strongly, but only very quickly, before they are gone again, replaced by the next thing, and the next. In all this, he is the opposite of Macbeth: he sleeps well, has no trouble praying and is not troubled by his conscience – and the reason is that he remembers nothing at all.

———

The reason we know about Macbeth's memory and the way it keeps him up at night is that he takes us into his confidence. There is another famous character, Wood writes, who is presented to us very differently. King David, as presented to us in the Bible, gives us no insight into his mental state. Instead, everything we know about him we learn from his actions. To us, he has no past, no inner life, no memory to trouble him. As a result, we cannot entirely understand him. David is 'opaque to us, one feels, precisely because he is transparent to God, who is his real audience'. At one point, Wood writes that 'despite the many revelations and subtleties of the Old Testament narrative . . . David remains a public character'.

As I read these pages about King David, I felt a sharp and sudden recognition, similar to the jolt I had felt upon first reading the work of T.M. Luhrmann: here was the man I had been writing about. When I came across that last passage, in particular, something in my chest leapt: *here was Scott Morrison*. Despite everything, despite the immense dramas of his brief time in the prime ministership, he *remains a public character*. David 'sees, and acts. As far as the narrative is concerned, he does not think.' Morrison is a practical man, who will not conduct himself as though he's sitting on Oprah's couch. We know him from his actions, but that is as far as we are allowed to go. Perhaps we might understand more if we could understand his faith, but he does not intend to justify his faith to us, which really means he intends to justify nothing at all.

At some point, the construction of a self for public consumption – a task in which we are all constantly engaged – may become difficult to untangle from the actual self. Morrison's tendency to turn away from the past and towards the present, over and over, with no sign of remembering what has come before, might at one point have been merely a useful strategy for public presentation; or perhaps, more likely, the tendency was there and became more pronounced with time as Morrison found a use for it, the way we all lean on our native talents. In either case, it seems unlikely that anyone could maintain such behaviour, across so many years, if it were not a central aspect of their experience of the world.

———

In 1988, the commentator Michael Kinsley defined a 'gaffe' as 'when a politician tells the truth – some obvious truth he isn't supposed to say'.

One of the truly remarkable facts about Scott Morrison is how few gaffes there have been in his career. He makes mistakes, says things that are obviously false, even lies, but rarely does he say something that makes you think that you are suddenly, briefly, getting a glimpse of something you were not meant to see.

In 2015, Tony Abbott, Peter Dutton and Morrison were standing in a room, waiting for a meeting to begin. Abbott had just returned from Port Moresby, in Papua New Guinea. Dutton made a joke about the meeting running to 'Cape York time'. Abbott said they'd had a bit of that in Port Moresby. Dutton said time didn't mean anything when you were about to have water lapping at your door.

These were insensitive and racist jokes, and the three men were political professionals: a prime minister and two men who wanted to be prime minister. Only Morrison noticed the boom microphone that was dangling above their heads. He did not laugh at the jokes; then, casually turning away from the conversation, mentioned it to both men, not looking up, in order not to draw the attention of anyone else in the room to the information he was imparting. In this public forum, two men believed that what they were saying was private. The third man would never make this mistake.

I find myself wondering if there is much left of Morrison's private self at all: if the public man has, over the course of years, slowly crowded out the private man, the way an ambitious employee might gradually usurp the responsibilities of his superior. If that sounds like an extreme assertion, it is worth pausing for a moment to consider the idea that this is, increasingly, the case for many of us: that the part of us that publicly performs has, in recent years, threatened to outgrow the part of us that is private. Through Facebook and Twitter and Instagram and TikTok, most of us are performing for an obvious audience some of the time. Without us paying much attention, that 'some of the time' can easily become 'most of the time'. We might find ourselves constantly thinking in the form of potential tweets or seeing the world as a series of Instagrammable images – I have found myself doing both at different times. It is not much of a stretch to imagine a politician following a similar path.

A purely Machiavellian figure might pursue such a strategy for the political benefits it brings – perfection of the performance, and a lowering of the chances of ever being caught out – and certainly Morrison is both ambitious and calculating. Possibly, though, it is just as much a defensive strategy, taken up by somebody intensely private, desperately fearful of having his private self discovered and displayed. It is impossible to know – it is likely Morrison does not himself know – what precisely drives his unending quest to ensure that nobody outside his immediate family can reach beyond the surface he allows to be shown to the world, but it is worth observing that artists of various sorts – actors, comedians, authors – are often similarly private. Spending so much of their lives baring their souls, they feel the importance of walling off some part of themselves. This attempt usually fails, because the nature of the careers they have chosen is that the private and the public cannot be separated, however much they wish it; an artist who does not show her soul produces only empty work.

———

In truth, we are bored by Scott Morrison not because we know enough about him, but for the opposite reason: we know nothing important about Morrison the man at all. We know nothing of his inner self, nothing about his beliefs, and the few things he says that indicate emotion are almost impossible to square with what he has actually done.

This seems, to me, intimately connected with Morrison's failure to speak in clear language. In an analysis of the work of novelist Kazuo Ishiguro – whose books include *The Remains of the Day* and *Never Let Me Go* – James Wood writes that characters are often repressing something unpleasant, like their complicity with fascist politics. 'They misread the world because reading it "properly" is too painful. The blandness of Ishiguro's narrators is the very rhetoric of their estrangement; blandness is the evasive truce that repression has made with the truth.'

That a flat character will eventually bore us was an argument made by the inventor of the concept, E.M. Forster. He acknowledged that there are times when flat characters appear to vibrate, to join the ranks of genuine people, as in Dickens. But for the most part, he said, flat characters, with their repetitive behaviours and repetitive speech, are only pleasing if they are comic. A flat character who is serious or tragic is likely only to bore us, because their repetitions do not point to any deeper facts about themselves or humanity.

This is the case for Morrison. The elements of his 'character' that we know about are only superficial. We know he likes a curry; we know that he likes rugby league. 'Pragmatic' comes closer to telling us something, but not very much closer, because the word itself is empty, a description in the negative rather than the positive: it tells us he will not die in a ditch, not what he might die in a ditch for.

A COUNTRY

TOGETHER

In the fifth week of his prime ministership, Scott Morrison posted a tweet accompanied by a picture of two blue thongs. The thongs were painted with white stars and the Union Jack, to represent the Australian flag. They were propped upright in sand, the ocean behind them.

The tweet read:

> Indulgent self-loathing doesn't make Australia stronger. Being honest about the past does. Our modern Aus nation began on January 26, 1788. That's the day to reflect on what we've accomplished, become, still to achieve. We can do this sensitively, respectfully, proudly, together.

It was accompanied by a link to an article in *The Daily Telegraph*, in which the picture appeared. The story reported that the Byron Shire Council had decided to hold its citizenship ceremonies not on Australia Day, but the evening before.

This might seem like an innocuous shift – but there was a political charge to it. The council wanted to make the change to acknowledge that Australia Day itself – which marked when Arthur

Phillip, commander of the First Fleet, stepped ashore in Sydney Cove – was the date 'the cultural decimation and denigration of the First Australians began'. This was the indulgent self-loathing Prime Minister Morrison was so annoyed about.

So began that year's version of what seemed to be becoming a new Australian political tradition. It should be odd for a major newspaper to focus on the activities of a single council, and odder still for a prime minister to weigh in. But it was predictable enough: Malcolm Turnbull had inaugurated the practice the year before, attacking another council for something similar. Morrison was merely following the play. Byron Shire Council had to be stopped.

Morrison's tweet was not impulsive. The story in the *Telegraph* was three days old. On the same day the tweet was posted, the prime minister gave quotations to *The Courier-Mail*, and provided a column in his name. Most of it was just a longer version of that tweet – but there was a surprise at the end. He suggested that a separate occasion be set aside to honour and acknowledge Indigenous Australians. 'That is a topic for another day.'

As anyone could have predicted, the topic instead arose again immediately, when Morrison, who had made himself available to the media, was asked about the column that had appeared in that morning's papers. 'I have said just today that it would be good to have a chat about it. We should think about it,' he said.

The interviewer said, sensibly enough, 'But I guess, Mr Morrison, we've been talking and maybe arguing about another Indigenous day for several years now. So to put this out in the public arena, haven't you got an idea for another date?'

'Well, I've got some private thoughts but I'm more interested to know what other Australians think,' Morrison replied.

Then he mentioned the anniversary of the 1967 referendum, in which Australians had voted for Indigenous people to be included in the census of Australians – in other words, for their right to be counted as Australians. 'I mean, that's a pretty significant day, I think, for Indigenous Australians. But it is not a day for being down in the mouth.'

The interviewer asked if that day should be a public holiday. That was a matter for the states and territories, came the reply. Morrison ended with this upbeat message:

You don't have to drag some people down to lift others up. It's the same when I talk about tax. Why do you have to tax people more to tax others less? That's not how you bring Australians together. I want to bring Australians together about this, not drive them apart.

It was a strange incident. The prime minister of the country had made a suggestion of national significance, and then said now was not the time to discuss it. When asked about his grand proposal, it seemed he'd barely thought about it.

———

In spirit, Morrison's attack on the Byron Shire Council stretched back at least to John Howard's attacks on 'black armband' history – a phrase that came from the historian Geoffrey Blainey, who contrasted it with the 'three cheers' approach – and specifically to a lecture Howard gave in 1996. Howard described the challenge

> to ensure that our history as a nation is not written defini-
> tively by those who take the view that we should apologise for
> most of it. This black armband view of our past reflects a
> belief that most Australian history since 1788 has been little
> more than a disgraceful story of imperialism, exploitation,
> racism, sexism and other forms of discrimination. I take a
> very different view. I believe that the balance sheet of our his-
> tory is one of heroic achievement and that we have achieved
> much more as a nation of which we can be proud than of
> which we should be ashamed.

In his maiden speech, Morrison had seemed to reject Howard's
view. The first time I read this passage I had been impressed; here
was a man, I'd thought, who felt deeply that wrongs had been
done and wanted to speak about those matters with nuance. Here
is the text:

> I do not share the armband view of history, black or other-
> wise. I like my history in high-definition, widescreen, full,
> vibrant colour. There is no doubt that our Indigenous pop-
> ulation has been devastated by the inevitable clash of cultures
> that came with the arrival of the modern world in 1770 at
> Kurnell in my electorate. This situation is not the result of
> any one act but of more than 200 years of shared ignorance,
> failed policies and failed communities. And we are not alone:
> our experience is shared by every other modern nation that

began this way. There is much for us all to be sorry for. Sadly, those who will be most sorry are the children growing up in Indigenous communities today, whose life chances are significantly less than the rest of us.

We can choose to sit in judgement on previous generations, thinking we would have done it differently. But would we? Hindsight is a wonderful thing. Nor can we compare the world we live in today with the world that framed the policies of previous generations. So let us not judge. Rather, having apologised for our past – as I was proud to do in this place yesterday – let us foster a reconciliation where true forgiveness can emerge and we work together to remove the disadvantage of our Indigenous communities, not out of a sense of guilt or recompense for past failures but because it is the humane and right thing to do. Having said this, we cannot allow a national obsession with our past failures to overwhelm our national appetite for celebrating our modern stories of nationhood. We must celebrate our achievements and acknowledge our failures at least in equal measure. We should never feel the need to deny our past to embrace our future.

Reading this a second time, and paying more attention, I found my admiration faded. The more time I spent with the passage, the more Morrison's words seemed like confused mush. Like his comments on Australia Day, the text was nothing more than a series of attempts to take every possible position. What I had mistaken for nuance was in fact a refusal – or perhaps an inability – to say anything clear.

The day before this maiden speech, the Labor prime minister, Kevin Rudd, had apologised to Indigenous Australians for the laws and policies of governments over many years, and especially for the removal of children from their families. This was an acknowledgement of specific sins, done by specific people. Morrison declared he was proud to have been part of that apology. But if you look at his own language, it is unclear what he thought he was apologising for. There was devastation – but it was not caused actively, by someone, but only passively, by the 'inevitable clash of cultures'. If there was any blame to go around, it seemed, from his reference to 'shared ignorance', that it lay equally with Indigenous people. The same thing happened everywhere in the world, he said, seeming to excuse it altogether. Then he said there was much for us all to be sorry for, which sounded a lot like Morrison was repeating his point about shared blame – but this was unclear, because Morrison left even the word 'sorry' in a fuzzy and confused state, saying, in his next breath, that those who would be most sorry were Indigenous children.

We have here the reverse of Malcolm Turnbull's final press conference, which seemed clear only afterwards. What Morrison says often sounds, at first, like it means something. Instead, you realise afterwards that it means nothing at all; or, rather, that each sentence expresses a different position, so that by the end it is likely, if you are so disposed, to come away believing that Morrison agrees with you, whatever your position happens to be. This may be deliberate. It is also possible that it represents Morrison's best attempt at considered thought.

A maiden speech is often taken as a concise encapsulation of a politician's outlook on the world; a pure expression of their actual self before the deadening effect of party politics and the need to please their seniors overwhelm them. Morrison's speech is not concise; rather than clarity, it offers confusion. In this, it is just as much a classic maiden speech as any other – because this is Morrison, exactly. As so often in Morrison's career, there is a sense that nobody, finally, is responsible. Bad things seem simply to happen, without the clear intention of anyone involved. If you go looking for solid meaning, something to tell you what he thinks about the world, you will be disappointed. It is like trying to grab at empty air.

———

Such foolishness is, perhaps, harmless enough, in so far as it is mindless. Less harmless was the dishonesty in Morrison's defence of the date of Australia Day in those 2018 interviews. Repeatedly, he said that you couldn't pretend Australia hadn't changed on 26 January. Nobody was asking anybody to pretend such a thing. Instead, many Indigenous people were saying, far more simply, that it was not a date they found easy to celebrate – it was a day they mourned precisely because Australia had changed. Their point was the opposite of what Morrison pretended it was.

Morrison said it was a day to celebrate all Australians – you didn't need to drag others down to raise other people up. This was another straw man. Who was saying that anybody should be dragged down? And who were these people who might *be* dragged down? Captain Arthur Phillip, dead for 200 years?

Morrison was inventing threats where there were none. He was imputing to Indigenous people some phantom desire to denigrate other Australians, and giving those other Australians a reason to be angry at Indigenous people. He was doing exactly what he had explicitly warned others against doing: tearing one group down and setting Australians against each other.

This was insulting – as was Morrison's childish language as he sought to minimise the murders and massacres:

You look at your own life's experience, you look at the whole thing. You don't pretend your birthday was on a different day. What you do is you look at your whole life's experience. Your achievements and a few scars from some mistakes and things that you could have done better.

By the next day, his language had become more confused and child-ish still, the proposal even weaker:

We can't turn our back on our history, but equally we don't have to be down in the mouth about it all the time either . . . We have NAIDOC Week and a lot of people have said, yeah, we've got a lot of these. And so let's just look at it and are we doing something which sufficiently acknowledges the great contribution and success of our Indigenous peoples? Some may say yes, some may say no. But I'll tell you, one thing is for certain, Australia Day ain't changing.

In that interview, Morrison was also asked about the Uluru Statement from the Heart, then a year old. With no preamble, Morrison – perhaps to placate the members of his party upset by his proposal for a new Indigenous day – stated his position: 'I don't support a third chamber.'

The Uluru Statement from the Heart had been agreed upon, after formal discussions lasting two years, at a meeting of Indigenous people near the great and sacred rock Uluru, in the middle of a desert in the middle of Australia, on the fiftieth anniversary of the 1967 referendum. The statement connects present harm to ancient wrongs, and calls for redress and repair. One form that should take, the statement says, is a Voice for Indigenous Australians enshrined in the Constitution.

In the plainness of its language and the clarity of its arguments, the Uluru Statement from the Heart is one of the most beautiful documents in Australian history. It has the potential to be one of the most significant. Here is a small section (the full statement is less than 500 words long):

> Proportionally, we are the most incarcerated people on the planet. We are not an innately criminal people. Our children are aliened from their families at unprecedented rates. This cannot be because we have no love for them. And our youth languish in detention in obscene numbers. They should be our hope for the future.
>
> These dimensions of our crisis tell plainly the structural nature of our problem. This is *the torment of our powerlessness*.
>
> We seek constitutional reforms to empower our people and take *a rightful place* in our own country. When we have power over our destiny our children will flourish. They will walk in two worlds and their culture will be a gift to their country.

As prime minister, Morrison had not made clear his position on the Voice to Parliament. Now he had, with a lie the Liberal Party had started using the year before. The form of the Voice had not been determined, and many Indigenous people were keen to emphasise that it would have no legislative power – in other words, it would not have the power of the two chambers of parliament. It would advise – that was all. This was a crucial distinction.

By describing the Voice to Parliament as a 'third chamber', Morrison was perpetuating the lie that what had been asked for was some kind of separate vote, or veto power, for Indigenous Australians. It was a malicious lie, and if there were any suggestion of openminded generosity in Morrison's previous simplistic comments, it was banished now. By saying he did not support a third chamber, Morrison was repeating the tactic he had used to respond to the call to change Australia Day: misrepresenting what was being requested in order to refuse it.

———

Soon, it became clear there had been no need for any of these fervent and confused discussions, these misrepresentations of the sincere views of Indigenous people – like the fuss around strawberries, it had largely been for show. Morrison had accused the mayor of Byron Shire Council of treating Australia Day like a 'political football'. But it had been Morrison who had turned the issue – via a tweet, an interview, a column and a series of follow-up interviews – into the most prominent item on the political agenda for several days.

If Morrison, or someone in his office, had called the council – and, remember, three days had elapsed between the council's decision and Morrison's decision to weigh in – it could have been sorted out quite easily. On the same day that Morrison tweeted, someone at *The Australian* picked up the phone and called the mayor. He was unrepentant about his political views, but said that if the government refused the council's request, that would be the end of the matter – they would hold the citizenship ceremony on Australia Day after all. 'It'd be unfair to make new citizens drive 45km to the next municipality.'

PROUD

Melissa Mullens had gone for a swim at Shelly Beach wearing her yellow kangaroo-sign earrings and her blue Australian-flag cowboy hat. 'I wasn't going to go for a swim because I'm a beauty therapist and it's really important to protect your skin. But it's hot today and we really wanted to celebrate Australia Day so I left my hat on when I swam.'

Mullens was one of the Shire locals quoted in a *Daily Telegraph* story about Australia Day in 2019. The story began like this:

> As far as many Cronulla locals are concerned, Australia Day is the best day of the whole year.
>
> Bec Walker and her friends settled in early at Blackwoods Beach with flags, beach balls and picnics for her favourite day of the year.
>
> 'I love Australia Day, everyone gets the day off, everyone's happy and celebrating,' Ms Walker said.
>
> 'It brings everyone together.'

The article went on: 'The Prime Minister of the Shire had captive constituents screaming for ScoMo when he made a brief address.'

At the end of the speech, in which Scott Morrison acknowledged the nation's ancient history and its recent prosperity – to what the newspaper described as 'roars from the crowd' – he said, 'Today, all I can say is how good is the Shire, how good is Australia, and as always, up up Cronulla.'

In September 2018, a month after being sworn in as prime minister, Morrison attended a ceremony to mark the beginning of construction on a new airport. 'How good is this?' he said. Concluding the speech, he said, 'How good is this? How good is this?'

Two weeks after that, he said, 'How good is Queenstown?' Four days after that: 'To lead the best country in the world – how good is that?' Three days after that: 'The serious part of the job is a great privilege and you can make a difference every day – how good is that?'

He had first used the phrase as prime minister at a press conference where he gave two thumbs up when asked about the tennis player John Millman, who had just beaten Roger Federer. 'Mate, John Millman. How good is John Millman? I mean, how good.' Once he had started using the phrase, and until the election in May 2019, it appeared in official transcripts about three times a month.

The list of subjects that received the recognition included:

- Bernice who called in to 2GB
- the city of Parramatta
- the Seventh Brigade of the Australian Defence Forces
- Liberal MP Trevor Evans
- Aunty Violet and her Welcome to Country

- the mental health charity Headspace
- using Indigenous history to teach science
- the girls out there playing football and matching it up with the boys
- flood victims who donated from their emergency grants to bushfire victims
- mining
- the fact that we all get along as well as we do
- Sri Lankan curry.

Three times a month may not seem all that frequent – but we are only talking about Morrison's public speech, and then only those occasions his office transcribed. The phrase is overtly informal and colloquial; spoken by a prime minister, it stands out. It is a perfect vehicle for a branding exercise. It is also exactly what you would expect a flat character in a novel to do: repeat the same phrase, over and over. Morrison's ostentatious pride in his country is the over-egged aspect of his character that enables you to recognise him.

———

Two weeks before Australia Day 2019 – the spat with Byron Shire Council had happened four months earlier – Morrison made a new entry in his ledger of catchphrases. He announced that the government would now take steps to force every council in the country to hold their citizenship ceremonies on 26 January. Again, he accompanied his announcement with a column for the tabloid papers, this one about how much he had enjoyed his recent family holiday on the South Coast.

There was no sign of the angry mob on social and in other media, shouting at each other and telling us all what we're supposed to do, think and say. It was a great reminder that there are quite a lot of us who actually think Australia is a pretty great place and we don't really have too much time to be angry.

The column went on to outline the 'unshouted' views Morrison had picked up from 'us quieter Australians', who were 'thankful' – he did this, he wrote, as a balance to the 'angry noisy voices'.

Those 'unshouted views' were, for the most part, fairly meaningless platitudes, as you can tell from a potted summary Morrison gave that morning: 'I've always been clear where I stood, whether it's on family issues or whether it's on the rule of law or making sure we stand up for respect and integrity and all of these issues, a strong economy.'

These values are so vague and inoffensive that they are probably held by every Australian. Morrison, though, was intent on dividing the country in two. 'Quieter Australians' had now become 'quiet Australians', and the phrase turned up again in another interview that day. These, he said, were the Australians he was focused on, which came with an implied division: he was not focused on the others.

———

By the time a phrase becomes commonplace, it can seem harmless; we no longer notice it. This does not mean that the phrase has shed its meaning. Instead, the meaning, with its repetition, has sunk into the marrow of public life.

The phrase 'working families', for example, the constant assertions that governments – including the Labor government I worked for – were governing with them in mind, emphasises, first, that families are the central unit of the nation, and second, that people who are working are at the centre of the government's thoughts. Some would say: well, we are all in families, aren't we? Where's the harm in that? But for me, when that phrase is uttered, I see an image in my mind's eye of a traditional nuclear family: at its vaguest, a grouping of parents and kids. I don't see single people; I don't think of the extended family; I don't think of couples without children; I don't think of the extended social groups that, for many people, come to replace family. Working families are no doubt the majority, and there is an obvious political imperative to convince the majority of voters that you are with them, but governing is – or should be – about something broader, and often the groups not in the majority are the ones that most need a government's help.

Morrison has tried to claim a Liberal lineage by comparing his phrase to Menzies' 'forgotten people'. There is similarity, in their attempts to turn frustration at being sidelined into proud identity – but the difference is significant. 'Forgotten' is a description of what has been done *to* those people, and seeks to rescue them from that denomination, restoring them to parity with those who have already been remembered. 'Quiet', on the other hand, is an affirming description of a choice they have made, and an encouragement to keep on making it. And where 'forgotten' seeks to rescue so that none might be forgotten, 'quiet' elevates Morrison's chosen people over other Australians, sets them in praiseworthy contrast with those who have made the opposite choice, to raise their voices.

The phrase itself is not original: it is a rephrasing of the more famous 'silent majority', which itself came from 'quiet Americans', a phrase made famous by US president Richard Nixon in a 1969 speech in which he warned of the danger when 'a vocal minority' took precedence over the 'silent majority'.

Nixon had begun making use of this sentiment during the campaign that made him president, though absent the specific phrase. One election ad, called 'Look at America', began with pictures of a city riot and flaming buildings. Sirens could be heard. The ad ran for four minutes, and included these lines: 'Let us listen now to another voice. It is the voice of the great majority of Americans – the non-shouters; the non-demonstrators. They are not racists or sick; they are not guilty of the crime that plagues the land.'

These people are defined, by Nixon as by Morrison, by what they are not. They don't shout or protest – but, the ad tells us, defensively, they are not racists either, and they are sick of being called racists simply because they say what they have always said, act as they have always acted. They don't want to change; they don't want the world to change; and they don't want to be criticised for not wanting change. It is a particular mix, of feeling comfortable with the way things are, but uncomfortable because there is always the chance that things are about to shift. It is both assured and defensive. In a wealthy country, like Australia now or America in the 1960s, these people will often be the majority – because why would they want anything to change? A prime minister who has no desire to do anything much fits them to a T.

The most significant trait here is a lack of anger – or rather, the determination not to show anger, the emotion most commonly associated with raised voices. Some identify a lack of anger with maturity, with adulthood. This has the ring of common sense. In fact, it falls down very quickly. Morrison has been happy to talk about anger, his own and that of others. It was, for example, his main justification for complaining about flying asylum seekers to the funerals of their family members: he was angry and understood the anger of others. Yet anger is something Morrison criticises.

What he really means is *anger directed at certain topics*. If you complain about asylum seekers and their funerals, or the decision of a local council about Australia Day, your anger is justified, even worthy of kicking off a national political debate. If you are angry about injustice towards certain groups that have suffered more than their share of injustice, then your anger is a sign that you should be dismissed.

———

The common element in Morrison's interventions in debates over our national culture is that they rely on the artificial creation of an enemy. Quiet Australians exist less as a group in themselves than in opposition to angry Australians. Morrison's defence of Australia Day is defined by what he won't do, what he doesn't believe should be done (tear others down). A 'third chamber' – that fictional creation of his colleagues – won't be granted, though nobody, in fact, asked for one. Morrison summons up shadows, then tells the nation he will fight them.

This is a consistent theme in Australian politics. Scott Morrison's hero, John Howard, by attacking the 'black armband' view of history, asked the nation to take pride in its past. This was not really a positive exhortation: it was, in essence, a position constructed in opposition to another view, which Howard presented not as what it was – a call for a more complex understanding of our history, with due attendance to the darker, violent chapters that until then had been often skipped past – but as a single-minded determination to recite a litany of shame. This case, made by eminent historians, was caricatured by Howard as reflecting 'an essentially negative, carping, mean-minded, mean-spirited view of what this country has achieved'.

Howard spent a significant period of his prime ministership transforming pride and shame from mere viewpoints into identities. The cartoon characters who held the 'black armband' view were the snobbish, elitist intellectuals. To have pride in your country and its past was to be an ordinary Australian.

He went further. By sustained and determined effort, Howard turned Australia Day and Anzac Day into symbolic performances of his side of the culture wars. The three elements were fused together. If you were ordinary, then you were proud of your country's past and waved flags as you celebrated it. When Howard, and later Turnbull, and then Morrison defended Australia Day from calls to change it, they were defending not so much a date or an idea of history as an identity, the *ordinary Australian* – the type of bloke who might drink a beer as he cooked a curry and watched the Sharks on TV. But where Howard, and even more so Turnbull, were defending others, the ordinary Australians they claimed to champion, Morrison was defending himself – and, even more importantly, the version of himself he had produced for public consumption.

———

The national pride of Australians is an odd thing. It is unmoored, free from any obvious anchoring fact. At school, Australian history was a subject we detested. This must have been the result of something other than the stories, which should have fascinated children: there was cruelty, and death, and gold, and theft, and battle. There is something in the air, when Australians talk of their history, a vague but encompassing boredom that prevents us from listening to the details.

What might our pride have attached to? Australia has never been an idea, the way the United States is. We have no great intellectual history to proclaim; our great novelists and intellectuals are individuals, not numerous enough to be anything other than *sui generis*; there are no enduring schools or literary groupings. We have had few enterprising businessmen, as in America, who have with the force of their will revolutionised the country: there is wide acceptance that we have become rich from our natural resources. This is not to say there are no reasons for pride, only that they are insufficiently unique to provide unselfconscious national mythology. We have contributed to wars, like every nation, and failed in several; we were early to democracy, but were not the earliest and, after all, democracy is no longer rare; 'mateship' is hard to define. Probably our greatest claim would be to have created a workers' paradise of sorts, but this is an uneasy topic for conservative prime ministers, and unions are hardly what they were. We are proud of our sporting achievements, but we know this is a thin fact on which to hang a national identity.

This is perhaps why men like Howard must work so hard to attack our shame: there are not sufficiently clear causes for pride to outweigh it. The scales are constantly poised to tip, and the fear that they will, once and for all, is in our hearts, which know the very real danger that if we spend too much time with our history, we will find plenty of reasons for shame. Even the part of our nation of which we are most proud – its natural beauty – is vexed, because it is tied to the original sin of theft and massacre: the land does not really belong to most of us.

I suspect this was part of the reason the history I – like the generation above me, including Scott Morrison – was taught bored us. It had to remain vague and uninteresting because there was so much specific, interesting and shameful that was not being mentioned, or at least not described in language that was accurate and forceful. Liars are advised not to use specific details, because they will linger in the mind and trip them up. The writers of our textbooks seem to have absorbed this advice unconsciously. The history we were taught was coated in a fog of blandness. Conflicts were rendered near invisible.

This tendency had been worse still in the past; then, the conflicts were even less visible. The anthropologist W.E.H. Stanner has described the 'cult of forgetfulness practised on a national scale', a phenomenon he rendered as 'the great Australian silence'. With time, and the work of Indigenous and non-Indigenous historians, actual silence became indefensible. It became the done thing to acknowledge that white Australians had not always acted perfectly; even Howard felt it necessary to acknowledge, in passing, the 'black marks' on our history.

As long as this was done only in passing, though, it could be contained, and easily outweighed by ostentatious pride. Today, our prime minister describes murder and genocide as 'some mistakes

and things that you could have done better'. We are back in the
territory of Kazuo Ishiguro: blandness as 'the evasive truce that
repression has made with the truth'.

———

When Australia Day itself arrived, and Melissa Mullens was bathing
with her blue cowboy hat and her yellow kangaroo-sign earrings,
Morrison's earlier vague proposal to create a new national day for
Indigenous Australians had been forgotten. Before he arrived in
Cronulla, to the roar of the crowd, he had held a press conference
in Canberra, where he was asked again about Indigenous requests
to change the date of Australia Day: 'For them it's a day of mourn-
ing. What do you say to Indigenous Australians who find today a
very difficult day, not a day for celebration?'

Morrison answered, 'Well, today is not a day for crab-walking
away from our history, as you heard me say today. I mean, 1788, 26th
of January for my ancestors, it was a pretty difficult day as well. They
came not by choice and in some pretty desperate circumstances.'

In other words, it was a particular part of our history that
Morrison did not want to crab-walk away from: the part that involved
his ancestors. Morrison was referring to the speech he had given earlier that day, in which he described their trials in great detail:

It was not a good day for my fifth great grandfather, William
Roberts. Bunkered down in the light-starved bowels of the
Scarborough with 207 other convicts, he had arrived in Port
Jackson after a long and treacherous voyage . . . It was a new
beginning for him, but it would have seemed a particularly

grim one at the time and life was indeed about to get a lot tougher . . .

When the *Scarborough* returned to New South Wales with the notorious Second Fleet, below deck on the *Neptune* was Kezia Brown . . . She was my fifth great grandmother . . . During her voyage, more than a quarter of the convicts died and over a third were hopelessly sick when they landed, with 124 to die soon after arriving.

The Rev Richard Johnson reported the misery of the scene of their arrival as 'indescribable . . . their heads, bodies, clothes, blankets, were all full of lice. They were wretched, naked, filthy, dirty, lousy, and many of them utterly unable to stand, or even to stir hand or foot'.

This is an emotive and gripping account of the trials faced by white Australians on arrival in this country. In the same speech, there are, if we are being generous, four references to the Indigenous suffering that was the result of that arrival. One is the single word 'resilience'. There are two references to the abstract and imper-sonal 'cruelties and dispossession of empire'. The other is this line: 'We can be so proud of our national story. Sure, it is not perfect, but no country is.'

Morrison's odd defensiveness about the difficulties his family faced, his insistence that these should be seen alongside the murder of Indigenous people – even, judging by his speech, elevated above those murders – has a long pedigree in this country. The historian Ann Curthoys has written:

Many non-indigenous Australians . . . see themselves as victims, not oppressors. In non-indigenous Australian popular culture, people see themselves as victims of large economic forces, middle class elites, and powerful nations overseas. Australian popular historical mythology stresses struggle, courage, and survival, amidst pain, tragedy, and loss. There is a special charge associated with the status of victim in Australian historical consciousness, and it is notable how good non-Aboriginal Australians are at memorialising their own sufferings.

Before Morrison became prime minister, it had become customary for leaders to give an acknowledgement of country – the Indigenous land on which they stood – before delivering a speech. For the first time in public life, there was a clear and consistent recognition of the special status of Indigenous people, the importance of their relationship to the land and the fact that it was theirs. When Morrison became leader, he added something: he delivers the acknowledgement, but each time he also acknowledges military veterans, and serving men and women, and thanks them for their service.

Anzac Day – which Morrison describes as 'our most sacred day' – memorialises, largely, the suffering of non-Indigenous Australians. In Morrison's version, so does Australia Day: it honours the sufferings of the convicts. The reason these stories of suffering can be told is twofold. First, because they belong to white Australians. Second, because they can be placed within narratives of progress, in which success is ultimately achieved, with the suffering not a miserable fact on its own but a necessary trial along the way to greater glory.

A white prime minister determined to present a triumphalist version of white Australian history cannot easily do this with the suffering of Indigenous Australians, who remain likely to die well before their non-Indigenous peers, more likely to see their children suffer from disease, more likely to be arrested for trivial offences and to die in prison. The pain of being colonised – unlike the pain of the colonisers – did not last for a few years and then end. It continued, and continued, and continues still.

When Morrison defended Australia Day, just after coming to office, on the basis that 'you don't have to drag some people down to lift others up', it was not clear who precisely was being dragged down. Read in the context of the speech he gave a few months later, on Australia Day itself, the answer becomes obvious. For Morrison, Australia Day is personal. Calls to change the date of Australia Day he takes as personal insult, because it is, in his mind, his ancestors who are being dragged down, whose great achievements are being neglected. When he talks about the progress the nation has made, he means the progress that his family, arriving here as convicts, fought for, and which has culminated in the election of their descendant to the highest office in the land. The story of Australia since 1788 is, in his mind, Morrison's own story. Australia Day is his day.

SECURE

In February 2019, just three months before the election, a headline on the SBS News website spoke of 'Morrison's fury'.

Scott Morrison's government had just lost a vote in the House of Representatives. This occasionally happens on trivial matters. It rarely happens on matters of substance. There were suggestions it might be grounds on which to call an election – an idea the prime minister rejected. 'This is a stupid bill,' he explained before the vote. 'It's written by people who haven't got the faintest idea how this works. We do, and I am so appalled that the Labor Party would even play this sort of political game to get a cheap vote in the House next week.' He would, he declared, 'simply ignore it'. The Opposition leader could 'take a running jump'.

About five years earlier, when Morrison was still immigration minister, a 24-year-old man, detained by Australia on Manus Island, had gone to see the nurse. He had a runny nose, a sore throat, fever, chills and aches. He also had a small lesion on his leg.

At first, Hamid Kehazaei's condition improved. By the next afternoon he was shivering and vomiting. His blood pressure began to drop, while his heart rate climbed, as did his temperature. By that evening he needed a wheelchair to get to the bathroom.

The next day, a transfer to the hospital at Port Moresby was requested. It was not seen by the responsible bureaucrat for several hours, because she was in meetings. Her reply came back after the last commercial flight had left for the day, requesting more information: 'I am wondering why this can't be managed at Lorengau hospital?' After receiving that information, the bureaucrat sent an email to her superior, but he had gone home and did not read the email for thirteen hours. By then, doctors had realised that the young man needed treatment in Brisbane; knowing that the departmental bureaucrats would be reluctant to agree, they continued to request a transfer to Port Moresby.

The transfer was granted. Kehazaei's skin had turned a 'grey purpley colour', what one doctor described as 'the most awful colour that I'd ever seen a human being'. In Port Moresby, his pupils were large, seemingly blind to the world. One witness, a doctor, said he believed the ventilator there was not working, and that an intravenous drip was inserted beside the vein, not in it. The 24-year-old suffered several heart attacks. Finally, he was flown to Brisbane, where he was placed on life support. He died a few days later.

The coroner later found that if Hamid Kehazaei had been transferred directly to Australia, he would likely have survived. There was a series of clinical errors: the care he had received was inadequate. The transfer process, the coroner said, was confusing; damningly, he said that while medical staff were focused on health, the bureaucrats were focused on 'bureaucratic and political imperatives' to keep the patients out of Australia.

Just before the man's death, the immigration minister, Scott

Morrison, questioned about the events, told *The Guardian*, 'When someone becomes ill they receive outstanding care.'

————

In the years since Hamid Kehazaei's death, the situation had not improved much. Increasingly, it seemed, children were suffering: despairing and depressed, they were refusing food and water. *The Guardian* reported: 'The current crisis on the island is overwhelming medical staff, who are referring dozens of children for transfer off the island, only to have their decisions rebuffed.'

The law that Prime Minister Morrison was now so furious about was an attempt to fix these problems. The new legislation – known as 'Medevac', short for 'medical evacuation' – prescribed that doctors, rather than bureaucrats, would have the authority to decide whether an asylum seeker needed urgent medical care. The government argued that this meant dangerous people would be allowed to come to Australia – even though the minister, under the new law, still had the power to block people on the basis of national security concerns or serious criminal records.

It argued, too, that the boats would start again. Because asylum seekers who had been allowed to fly to Australia for medical reasons sometimes launched legal challenges around their asylum status – in order to be allowed to stay in Australia – people smugglers would use this to argue that Australia's borders had weakened, and refugees would flock to our shores. This was a stretch. The argument required several logical steps: refugees would need to hear about the policy, and then get on boats hoping they might (a) become sick enough to be declared an emergency case by a doctor, necessitating their being flown to the mainland, and then (b) successfully mount a legal case that allowed them to stay.

Even if you could convince yourself that this sequence of steps was likely, there was a larger problem with the argument: the new law applied only to asylum seekers who had already arrived. At a press conference, Katharine Murphy pointed this out.

Morrison responded:

No, I'm sorry, Katharine, you fail to understand that people smugglers don't deal with the nuance of the Canberra bubble. They deal with the psychology of messaging, of whether things are stronger or whether things are weaker. It might be all fine and nice to talk about these nuances here in this courtyard. But when you're in a village in Indonesia and someone is selling you a product, there's no protections or truth-in-advertising laws for people smugglers. They just sell the message. What Tony Abbott has said is exactly what the people smugglers will be saying. Sorry, I'm going over here.

MURPHY: Prime Minister, it's not a nuance, it's a fact. And if I may –

PRIME MINISTER: It is a nuance which the people smugglers will ignore. What is true today Katharine, what is true today is as a result of what happened in the Parliament yesterday and what is happening in the Senate now, is our border protection laws are weaker than they were two days ago. That's a fact.

Morrison was applying a marketing man's expertise to what he said was largely a marketing operation. Some had enjoyed the irony of Morrison's different careers: as a tourism guy, he had wanted boats to come; now he wanted them to stop. This joke missed the deeper truth, which was that Morrison saw both jobs through the same lens: each was a question of marketing. Now, Morrison was telling the assembled journalists that what the law actually did mattered less than what people smugglers would say it did.

This was similar to the logic that had allowed ScoMo the character to take the place of whoever was there before. If a fiction was put forward strongly enough, then it could take the place of fact. This was the central, unspoken aspect of Morrison's political career, and so it was interesting that he was now saying the same thing quite openly: in the face of effective marketing, reality itself – the facts that Murphy was attempting to insist upon – fell away.

This became clearer still in what Morrison did next. Responding to his parliamentary defeat on the Medevac legislation, Morrison announced that the Christmas Island detention centre would be reopened – both to deal with the flood of arrivals the government was hysterically predicting, and so that sick asylum seekers could be treated within the new law but without being taken to the mainland. He would, he said, be engaging in some 'very clear messaging that my government is in control of the borders'.

Morrison flew to Christmas Island to reopen the detention centre himself. He took members of the media with him. The reopening, with the reinstatement of staff and security, cost $180 million. Two months later, it was revealed that the government intended to close the centre in July, after the election. Many people used the Medevac legislation, which had been passed – under its authority, at least 150 people were transferred to the mainland for urgent care – but there was never any flood of boats. Even after the election, the government continued to try to scare people about the coming impact. It never came.

The reopening of Christmas Island had been another show staged by the prime minister. Reality was being slowly crowded out by the images that Morrison chose to present.

———

Like all good shows, the Christmas Island extravaganza depended for its effect on a convincing villain.

An argument made by politicians across the political spectrum in recent years is that the boats must be stopped because of the threat of drowning. I suspect that this argument is made with varying degrees of sincerity. Still, it is not the main argument they offer; it is only the excuse offered, where necessary, to defend the worst abuses. The main argument is far simpler, and you can observe it in Morrison's description of the Medevac dispute: soon, he said, 'Australians will be deciding once again – as they did in 2013, as they did in 2001 – about whether they want the stronger border protection policies of . . .'

The months leading to the 2001 election – that Morrison now referred to – were marked by a series of events that brought the issue of national security to the fore. First, the prime minister, John Howard, forced a Norwegian container ship, the MV *Tampa*, carrying 433 refugees it had rescued from a stranded boat, to leave Australian waters. A month after that, there was another crisis around a different boat: the government falsely claimed that refugees had thrown their children into the water. Between these two moments of high national drama, the planes hit the Twin Towers in New York. The three issues blurred, leaving a disturbing series of overlapping impressions encouraged by the government: evil refugees, the type of people who would throw their children into the water, had to be stopped, lest they bring terror to our shores.

At this time in his own prime ministership, Morrison was speaking to Howard every week or two – sometimes more often. In 2001, as director of the Liberal Party in New South Wales, Morrison had, according to conservative columnist Miranda Devine, come up with Howard's election slogan – 'Certainty. Leadership. Strength'. Apparently, he kept a poster from that campaign in his office as 'an inspiration for his upcoming electoral battle'.

It made sense, then, for Morrison to do what Howard had done: find a way to cast refugees as outside the moral community that Australians stood firmly inside. Soon enough, with the election in prospect, he used the debate over the Medevac legislation to do just that: 'They may be a paedophile, they may be a rapist, they may be a murderer, and this bill would mean that we would just have to take them.'

'Strong borders' are, when you live on an island, abstractions – imaginary lines drawn on literally shifting seas. The vague phrase is of course a euphemism, meaning 'we are very good at keeping people out'. When is this an important skill? When the people to be kept out pose some threat. The beauty of 'strong borders' is that it says all of that in two words.

———

A month after Morrison had reopened the Christmas Island centre, a terrorist attack was committed by an Australian. It was not the first of Morrison's term. That had occurred late the previous year, when a man drove to the centre of Melbourne's CBD and, having set his car – a blue ute – on fire, began stabbing people. He was apprehended but died soon after, as did one of the three people he attacked. The attack was inspired by Islamic State.

The next day, Morrison held a press conference. He praised the 'brave and passionate' Islamic Australians who only wanted the best for their communities. He also – and this, of course, was what made headlines – seemed to blame Islamic leaders. There was 'a special responsibility on religious leaders to protect their religious communities and to ensure that these dangerous teachings and ideologies do not take root here. They must be proactive, they must be alert and they must call this out, in their communities and more broadly for what it is.' The implication, that Islamic leaders should identify potential offenders and stop them, was odd, because in the case that was being discussed, it was government authorities that had known about the attacker but failed to stop him: he was one of 230 Australians whose passports had been cancelled on ASIO advice, lest they travel overseas to fight for terrorist groups.

Three months later, Morrison delivered a speech focused on security. He introduced the section dealing with terrorism with reference to just one, specific type: 'radical extremist Islamist terrorism'. A month after Morrison's security speech, another attack occurred. It was far, far larger than the Melbourne attack. It was not in Australia – it was in Christchurch, New Zealand – but the terrorist was Australian. His name was Brenton Tarrant, and he was white.

Tarrant attacked two mosques in one day, killing fifty-one people, every one of them a Muslim. Morrison described the attack
frankly and accurately, calling it a 'vicious and callous right-wing
extremist attack' on Islamic people. He had another strong statement to make: 'These people don't deserve names. Names imply
some sort of humanity and I struggle to find how anyone who
would engage in this sort of behaviour and violence . . . He's not
human. He doesn't deserve a name.'

This strategy, of refusing to name terrorists, has spread in
recent years. It is not partisan: the left-wing prime minister of New
Zealand, Jacinda Ardern, took this approach to Tarrant too. In an
examination of Anders Behring Breivik, a far-right Norwegian terrorist, the novelist Karl Ove Knausgård wrote: 'Every time his name
appears in public, he gets what he wants, and becomes who he wants,
while those whom he murdered, at whose expense he asserted himself, lost not only their lives but also their names – we remember his
name, but they have become numbers.' Knausgård, however, follows
that long sentence with this short one: 'And yet we must write about
him, we must think about the crisis that Breivik's actions represent.'

There has never been any great effort in Australia to discuss the
crisis that the actions of this Australian might represent.

Racism is a powerful political force in Australia – as it is in many
countries – encouraged by prominent media figures and important
politicians. We know that Tarrant was active on the social media
sites of several far-right Australian groups. Those groups, in turn,
had interacted with prominent Australian politicians, including
George Christensen, an MP in Morrison's government, and Mark
Latham, a former leader of the Labor Party.

It is at least plausible – it should at least be the subject of searching discussion – that Australian culture might have played some role in the formation of this man's political mentality. If we can accept that, then perhaps we can recognise, too, that Australian culture did not simply spring into being in the past decade or so: it is the product of all the events that came before. The author Jeff Sparrow has connected the massacre to Australia's history, in an analysis of the New Zealand Royal Commission's findings on the atrocity:

> The report's authors tell us the perpetrator 'began expressing racist ideas from a young age, including at school and when referring to his mother's then partner's Aboriginal ancestry'.
>
> That should not surprise us. In the area where he grew up, a historian estimates that 'perhaps a fifth of the [Indigenous] population . . . were killed by guns and poison between 1838 and 1870'.

There is a more direct link to our contemporary political culture. Tarrant told the royal commission that he began to think politically, including worrying about immigration, at the age of twelve. Sparrow points out that this would have been in 2002, immediately after the *Tampa* election.

A man who kills Muslims may not seem to have much in common with the refugees who are often the victims of anti-Islamic sentiment. Our approach to them, however, is similar. By refusing to name the Christchurch killer, by presenting him as essentially inhuman, Morrison is doing with the murderer what he and Howard had earlier done with refugees. In both cases, they had been placed outside our moral community, their actions presented as incomprehensible to ordinary Australians. This is not merely a gesture of condemnation; it renders these people blank to us. It stops us treating their behaviour as human, which in turn prevents us from attempting to understand their behaviour at all.

And this, in turn, is another way of not asking questions about our own behaviour. The actions of refugees cannot be understood without some reference to our own actions: our participation in wars in Iraq and Afghanistan, our government's complicity with the Sri Lankan government, our failures as a member of the global community. Neither can Tarrant's behaviour be wholly separated from our own – but both life and politics are easier if we pretend that they can.

———

There is something in these connections that is a little too simple. There is no direct line of responsibility, no obvious relationship of cause and effect, between racism in Australian politics and a psychopathic act of terrorism. Yet I find myself unable to separate them entirely.

In the manifesto Tarrant left behind, he signed off like this: 'If I don't survive the attack, goodbye, godbless and I will see you all in Valhalla!'

You are not meant to take this very seriously. There is a lot in that manifesto that is not supposed to be taken seriously. It is full of jokes, and references to other in-jokes, jokes you will get if you are part of the community of young white men who spend an extraordinary amount of time online, reading and posting in forums for white nationalists and neo-Nazis.

White nationalism is a very strange beast these days – strange, that is, in unexpected ways. New followers are often recruited through jokes and memes, fed a steady stream of hate that seems light-hearted or ironic until they are full of the hate itself; or, if they were already full of hate, are clearer about the targets against which they should direct that hate. This is in line with much online culture, in which jokes dominate; also like much online culture, it both relies on and helps create an ironic distance between the people engaged in such behaviour and what that behaviour actually means.

Before Tarrant committed murder, he told people on 8chan, an online messageboard, that he would be streaming an 'attack'. Here is one description, from journalist Jason Wilson: 'The video live-stream of the killings tries to situate the terrible violence in a framework of irony, with references to subscribing to video game commentator PewdiePie, the game Fortnite, and a propaganda song performed by Bosnian Serb soldiers in the 1990s.'

A thick fog of bad faith hangs over all of this. Nobody is being entirely serious; the words do not mean what they appear to mean. Even the murderous actions are not entirely real: after the massacre, *The Sydney Morning Herald* reported that images from the killing had appeared on 8chan, altered to look as though they belonged to popular video games.

In his consideration of what might have allowed Breivik to commit his massacre in Norway, Knausgård writes about the necessary distance that must open up between one human and another to make killing possible – and the way that such a distance might appear in the midst of a society:

Five years before the massacre, Breivik isolated himself in a room at his mother's flat; he saw practically no one, refused visits, hardly ever went out, and just sat inside playing computer games, World of Warcraft mostly, hour after hour, day after day, week after week, month after month. At some point, this fantasy took over Breivik's reality, not because he experienced a psychotic break but because he discovered models of reality that were as uncomplicated and manageable as those of the game . . .

This is – as Knausgård observes – not unique to those who commit extremist acts of violence. The ability to blend fiction and reality, or to jump between the two, is an increasingly common aspect of the culture in which we all participate.

This is the most important understanding to bring to our interrogation of what Tarrant did. His murders are not a straightforward reflection of the racism we find in Australia; instead, they are a set of actions derived from a similarly distanced approach to the world. Racism creates distance between us and the world, by permitting the pretence that the people you are treating badly are not real people. Racism, like video games, and like the extremist violence that has become connected to both, offers an uncomplicated model of reality that comes to substitute for reality itself.

––––––––

If we have all become increasingly adept at setting up a separation between what is done or said and the meaning and impact of those actions – if we are all now practised in substituting our preferred realities for actual reality – you would expect this to be true of politics as well. And so it is: when Donald Trump came to power, we were told that the media had made the mistake of taking everything he said literally, but not taking him seriously. His supporters did the opposite: took him very seriously, but never literally. His words, we were assured, did not mean what they seemed to mean.

I have often heard friends question whether Andrew Bolt really believes the things that he says. Bolt is a right-wing commentator, at times verging on far-right, with a solid line in anti-Islamic sentiment. He often contradicts himself; he makes flagrant claims. It is a reasonable question, because Bolt is far from stupid, and is a skilful performer, flamboyant to a degree sometimes bordering on vaudevillian. Over the years, though, this question has come to seem to me a comforting alibi, a way for people to assure themselves that nobody so intelligent could believe such horrible things.

This is the way most of us watch politicians themselves. We see an elaborate and insincere performance. This is an alibi too, because we allow ourselves to believe that whatever our politicians do in our name, it is not entirely meant; it is just a part of the game they are playing. Their actions, and the consequences of their actions, vanish.

————

On the day that Morrison became prime minister, a court ordered that a girl be flown from Nauru to Australia. A source told *The Guardian*, 'She had a dream to be a doctor in Australia and to help others. Now, she is on food-and-fluid refusal and begging to die as death is better than Nauru.' Three doctors had recommended she be moved to Australia, but the government had not acted.

The intention behind the Medevac legislation was to intervene in matters of life and death. When Morrison lost the vote and the legislation passed, much of the analysis focused on the political effect of the new laws: what impact they would have on the next election. The suffering of real people vanished, replaced by discussion of the game of politics. Commentators for conservative newspapers lined up to declare that the apparent legislative defeat was a victory in disguise: it would entrench the view of Labor as weak on border protection. Joe Hildebrand wrote that Morrison might have just 'given himself his only possible chance of surviving as prime minister'. Miranda Devine, in an article that barely touched on the policy itself, judged that Morrison had inflicted a 'diabolical political wound on his opponents'. 'That', she declared, was 'how elections are won'.

RELAXED

In 2011, just after the funerals controversy, journalist Lenore Taylor reported in *The Sydney Morning Herald* that shadow ministers had been asked to bring three ideas for political attacks to a shadow cabinet meeting a few months earlier. Scott Morrison, she wrote, had 'urged the shadow cabinet to capitalise on the electorate's growing concerns about "Muslim immigration", "Muslims in Australia" and the "inability" of Muslim migrants to integrate'. Some of his colleagues were 'privately questioning whether he is trying to pursue an antiMuslim political strategy unilaterally'.

At the time, Morrison denied the story, though weakly. 'As all journalists know, I don't comment on shadow cabinet here or anywhere else. All I can say is the gossip reported today does not reflect my views.'

Shortly after the Christchurch massacre, respected commentator and media figure Waleed Aly, who is a Muslim, returned to the issue in a monologue on light current affairs show *The Project*. Aly said that he was gutted by the massacre – but he was not shocked, because the words in Tarrant's manifesto were so familiar. He proceeded to read the words of various Australian politicians. Among them, he included reports of the meeting in which a 'senior politician suggested his party should use community concerns about Muslims in Australia failing to integrate as a political strategy. That person is now the most senior politician we have.' This was a reference to Lenore Taylor's report on Scott Morrison.

Morrison's office called the offices of the network. There was, according to reporter Hamish Macdonald at *The Project*, a 'furious exchange'. Soon after, Morrison called the claim 'a disgraceful smear and an appalling lie'. *The Project* responded: Morrison had been offered the chance to respond to Aly's monologue in an appearance booked for that night. He had declined, and his office had cancelled his appearance entirely. (The government told reporters the appearance had never been confirmed.)

Morrison agreed to appear the following week. Aly began the interview by offering Morrison the chance to say what he wanted. The prime minister spoke of the horror and hatred on show in Christchurch, and of meeting with Islamic leaders in Australia: 'we hugged when we met, my friends and I'. He urged Australians to 'hug each other tonight. I think we need to keep hugging each other.'

Aly asked whether the Coalition had a problem with Islamophobia. Morrison said no, and that we should avoid jumping to conclusions about others. Aly listed examples of Islamophobia from within the government. Morrison said that he tried to lead by example, and asked, 'Do we want to get bogged down in this or do we want to move on to how we actually make things better?'

Soon, Aly gave Morrison a chance to do that. He asked about preferences at the next election, which was only months away. How would the Liberal Party be treating One Nation, the far-right party led by Pauline Hanson, which had started as anti-Asian and shifted, as the country's racist tastes changed, to opposing Islam? Would the Liberals be preferencing One Nation last?

Morrison would not answer – or, rather, he had several answers, none of which dealt with the question. Sometimes he said that preferences were decided by the party, which was technically true, but skipped over the fact that he was head of that party. Most times he said there would be no deals with One Nation – which was not an answer to the question.

Presumably Aly would have arrived at the topic, but the comments that Taylor had reported in 2011 were brought up first by Morrison: 'Waleed, the other night, you were very emotional . . .'

Morrison strongly denied the report. He said colleagues had denied it too. This was correct. There were several strong denials – though some accounts, too, were a little muddier than he would have liked. One of the colleagues Morrison cited said he couldn't remember. Another denied the story, but it turned out he hadn't been there. Malcolm Turnbull and Julie Bishop, who had been at the meeting, refused to comment. One minister's description of the meeting from 2011 emerged. 'Scott did talk about the strong feelings in the general community about Muslim immigration, and he said that we as a party had to engage with that sentiment. But I'm sure he meant we should engage in a constructive way.' Morrison said he had raised the issue, but his concern was to lower those concerns, not raise them.

———

To counter the idea that he was anti-Islam, Morrison brought up 'mateship treks', which he had been going on for years with Labor

MP Jason Clare, taking young Anglo Australians and Lebanese Australians to famous Australian military sites. The doctor and Islamic leader Jamal Rifi went with them to Kokoda. Rifi had criticised Morrison over the funerals attack, but continued to spend time with him publicly and privately. After the Aly interview, he described Morrison as a friend, and said, 'Pointing fingers at the prime minister and accusing him of hating Muslims is wrong. This man does not hate Muslims.'

These 'mateship treks' were spoken of as an act of healing after the racist Cronulla riots. The 2005 riots had begun after an altercation at North Cronulla beach between young people with Middle Eastern heritage and Anglo Australians. The powerful right-wing radio host Alan Jones told his listeners: 'My suggestion is to invite one of the biker gangs to be present in numbers at Cronulla railway station when these Lebanese thugs arrive.' He read out a message from an unidentified policeman: 'unfortunately the only language the Middle Eastern youth understand is a good hiding'.

The next weekend, 5000 people gathered at Cronulla beach. A young man of Middle Eastern heritage was attacked. People began to chant: 'We grew here, you flew here,' and 'Fuck off Lebs!' Sixteen people were arrested, and twenty-six were treated for injuries. That night there were revenge attacks – cars were smashed, people were assaulted and two men were stabbed. In one of the stabbing incidents, the attackers chanted, 'Get the Aussie dogs . . . get the Aussie sluts.'

In 2011, journalist Julia Baird put to Morrison that he had 'repeatedly defended Australians against charges of racism when this is brought into this debate. Look, given that in every country there are racist threads in public debate and in the community, what have you heard here that disturbs you? What have you found yourself correcting people on when it comes to the asylum seeker debate?'

Morrison tried to avoid answering, but Baird pressed him: 'So what has bothered you? I mean, as you've said, the Cronulla riots were in your own electorate, I mean, back in 2005.'

Morrison's answer was curious: 'Well, let me say, the Cronulla riots and the revenge attacks – the revenge attacks didn't occur in my electorate. They occurred up in Brighton-Le-Sands and Maroubra and other places. And, you know, people were stabbed in those revenge attacks.'

Baird pressed him a final time: 'I've just asked you twice about, are there elements of racism in the community which trouble you? I mean, is that not the mark of leadership, to also combat things that might be offensive or destructive or anathema to the Australian character?'

Morrison replied, 'I frankly don't waste a lot of my time dealing with extreme views.'

———

This habit – of seeking to ignore the more troubling narrative and then replace it with one that vindicates ordinary Australians – occurs again and again both in Morrison's career and in Australia's history. It even surfaces in perhaps the most famous book-length critique of Australia.

Reading Donald Horne's *The Lucky Country* is today a surprising experience, because of how accurately it still captures Australia and Australians – or at least a version of this country that still exists.

These are still perhaps the two most concise lines written to explain Australians: 'What they want they can usually get – a house, a car, oysters, suntans, cans of asparagus, lobsters, seaside holidays, golf, tennis, surfing, fishing, gardening. Life assumes meaning in the weekends and on holidays.' Some of these luxuries – *cans of asparagus!* – are now outdated. But the overall mentality remains, expressed best in John Howard's wish that Australians might feel 'relaxed and comfortable'.

Horne's book is most famous, now, for its title: 'the Lucky Country' is a term that has become commonplace. Know-it-alls are happy to explain to others that the title is often misapplied. Today we use 'the Lucky Country', mostly, to remind ourselves of the easy and beautiful lives many of us have here. Of course, it was intended by Horne as an excoriation of elites:

> Australia is a lucky country run mainly by second-rate people who share its luck. It lives on other people's ideas, and, although its ordinary people are adaptable, most of its leaders (in all fields) so lack curiosity about the events that surround them that they are often taken by surprise.

In later editions of the book, Horne would double down on this attack, adding to the list of leaders' sins the misuse of the title of his book: 'The long misuse of the phrase "the lucky country", as if it were praise for Australia rather than a warning, has been a tribute to the empty-mindedness of a mob of assorted public wafflers.'

Horne's emphasis on these mistakes as belonging only to 'public wafflers' is central to his analysis. He was eager, always, to stress that he had no criticism of the ordinary people of Australia – it was *only* the elites that he mistrusted. There was an obvious rebuttal of this separation, but Horne rejected it: the idea that elites 'cannot help being what they are because in an egalitarian country the elites are necessarily second-rate and necessarily reflect what is taken to be the mediocrity of the people' he attacked as 'fashionably gloomy'.

No doubt this feeling, in Horne, was genuine. It was also a convenient view: one that enabled him to launch a stinging and notorious attack while distancing himself from any suggestion of snobbishness. It is hard not to think that this unwillingness to broaden his critique – to consider also the possibility that the elements that so troubled him were common to both the elite and ordinary classes – was exactly what then allowed the country to go merrily on its way. After all, if we can contain our concerns to a small group of people who will be replaced soon enough, then our concerns are not really that concerning. No genuinely dramatic change need be considered, and certainly no intensive self-examination. The problem is always over there.

———

Horne's defence of Australians and their unconcerned temperament came, I suspect, from deep roots. He grew up in Muswellbrook, in the Hunter Valley north-west of Newcastle, but spent his childhood summers in Sydney. The four weeks from Christmas Eve onwards he spent in Cronulla. He wrote, in his first memoir, of heading to the beach twice each day. Members of their party would head into the surf, come back, describe their experience, then head back out again. Their skin would go crimson, then brown, then peel off in long, white strips. 'It was at Cronulla every summer that we bore witness to a truth that was self-evident to us every day of the year: the most important part of human destiny was to have a good time.'

Cronulla is one part of the Sutherland Shire, the area that Morrison represents in the Australian parliament, and in which he lives. It occupies a particular place in the Australian imagination. Nick Bryant, who wrote a detailed examination of the area in 2012, described the reality TV show *Sylvania Waters*, starring

> Noeline Donaher, a self-satirising blonde harridan, and her henpecked family. When casting the show, the British producer immediately latched on to them after discovering they owned a motor cruiser called *Blasé*. The viewer response in Britain to 'Mr and Mrs Australia', as the Donahers were dubbed, was so sneering that the *Sun* set up a hotline for readers to ring in and insult them. 'Meet Noeline,' it crowed. 'By tonight you'll hate her, too.'

Britain wasn't entirely wrong with its crowning of 'Mr and Mrs Australia'. Of course, a nation is hard to summarise, so it would be more precise to say that the Shire is the apotheosis of a particular version of the country – which is also the version of the country that Horne described in his famous book.

It is an area known for its outdoors, its beaches and its bush. It is known for being fairly white, in no small part due to the riots. Compared with the rest of the country, Shire residents are more likely to have been born in Australia, and to have two parents born in Australia.

Another statistic on which it departs from the average is its
wealth: it is richer than much of Australia, by a not insignificant
amount. On the other hand, it is not so far above the average as
to attract a reputation for ritziness – which is perhaps the most
emblematically Australian thing of all. The people who live there
have just enough reason to convince themselves they live like everybody else, just as Australia is a rich country that likes to pretend it
is full of ordinary working-class folk clinging to an old reputation
as a nation of beer-loving, footy-loving tradies.

   This sense of the country as clinging to some older idea of itself
helps make sense of Cronulla's appeal. Bryant cites an official history of the area from 1995 that asserts:

> The nearly 200,000 people who live there consider them-
> selves fortunate, and few would argue with them their way
> of life is as close as can now be achieved to what was once
> called the Australian Dream – the suburban home on its
> quarter-acre block, handy to the train to town, the beach
> and the bush.

That was written almost thirty years ago, but feels true today. The
dream is outmoded, of course, even in the Shire, where many, many
people live in apartment blocks, but it is *still* the Australian dream,
and essential to understanding the way we see ourselves and the
aspirations for ourselves that we retain.

   It is in fact the dream that Morrison himself has lived – an
extraordinary fact he presents as ordinary. He grew up in another
beachside suburb, and lived there for much of his life. The Morrisons'

three-bedroom house in the Shire has a swimming pool and sits on 696 square metres – not quite a quarter-acre, but not far off it.

Those who live in the Shire like to call it 'God's country'. They have a particular sense of pride in the place. Partly this comes from the area's role in Australian history: it is where Captain Cook, whose 'discovery' of Australia led to the colonisation of the country, landed. Partly it comes from the beauty of the area. Partly, one suspects, it comes from the sense that the area is bounded, in more ways than one. Bryant notes that 'nature has delineated its borders with unusual precision. Rivers, bays, the ocean and acres of thick bushland mark out its boundaries.' From the north, where much of Sydney is, you can only enter the Shire via bridges.

Perhaps most interestingly, there has seemed, over the years, to be little local interest in blunt discussion of the riots. Morrison, in his interview with Baird, was keen to avoid dwelling on them; he immediately shifted emphasis away from violence committed by white people in Cronulla to the violence committed against white people elsewhere. In his 2012 piece, Bryant wrote: 'While the vast majority of local residents shared the shock of the nation, more than six years on there is a palpable sense of denial about what the council prefers to call "the Cronulla disturbances".'

So the Shire is an area of high parochialism, cordoned off from the rest of the world by geography, and proud of its part in the history of colonisation. It is a rich area that doesn't think of itself as rich, an area with a famed history of racism that doesn't think of itself as racist, while clinging onto an outmoded view of itself built on nostalgia for a way of life that has passed. In all of this, it recalls the nation itself. And if the Shire represents Australia so perfectly, and Morrison represents the Shire so perfectly, then the next step is easy enough: Morrison represents Australia perfectly, or at least a certain version of Australia. It is possible to read that as a criticism, but Morrison would certainly say the same thing with pride.

————

There was no guarantee Morrison would represent the Shire – he almost did not. The ballot for Liberal Party preselection in the seat of Cook in July 2007 attracted strong candidates. Morrison was a former state director of the party. A barrister, Mark Speakman, ran – he went on to become the New South Wales attorney-general. An executive from Optus, Paul Fletcher, ran – he went on to become a federal cabinet minister. A magazine executive, David Coleman, ran – he became a federal minister too. Then there was a 31-year-old named Michael Towke, who ran a security business.

Towke had made a name for himself within the party by recruiting members to help Malcolm Turnbull when he wanted to run for parliament. He took those skills with him to the Shire, and surprised many when he decided to use his numbers to make himself the local MP.

It is not unusual for preselection battles to get dirty. This one was particularly dramatic. At the last minute, the vote was delayed. The matter had to be decided in the Supreme Court. Two weeks later, the vote went ahead. There were reports the prime minister, John Howard, was attempting to push Towke out. Towke threatened to take the matter to court and postpone the vote once again. The vote went ahead. Towke won. Morrison was knocked out in the first round; with 152 votes in play, he received just eight.

The Australian reported that some Liberals 'were celebrating the dismal performance of Mr Morrison'.

But the battle was not over. Before the vote, Towke had several times been asked to appear at the party's office and respond to allegations. Now these allegations began to appear in the media: Towke had been a member of the Labor Party; he had lied about his work history; he had not just recruited members, but paid their membership fees, which was against party rules. Some suggest there were worse rumours spread, on topics that might have been intended to implicitly raise concerns with voting members about Towke's ethnicity. There are suggestions his ethnicity was used directly as well: that an argument put to preselectors was that you just could not have a 'Leb' running in the Shire so soon after the Cronulla riots.

The drama continued. Towke was about to be endorsed when the state director intervened, apparently on behalf of Howard. There were reports Towke was about to stand down gracefully – but Towke, instead, said that he would fight. There were more leaks; another meeting was cancelled. Finally, in early August, the party executive voted. Towke was no longer the candidate. Two weeks later, with Towke no longer a threat, the executive affirmed that he was in fact 'a fit and proper person pursuant to the provisions of its constitution', noting the 'difficult time experienced by him, his family and supporters', and the 'unwarranted, unnecessary and often inflammatory' attacks on his character.

A week after that, Morrison won a new vote and was preselected.

Later, Towke began defamation proceedings against the publisher of *The Daily Telegraph* over articles written about him during the dispute. The company offered $110,000 and a private apology if the matter was kept confidential. Towke refused. 'These stories sent my mother to hospital,' he told conservative columnist Paul Sheehan. 'They demonised me . . . I was willing to bankrupt myself to clear my name.' News Limited then offered $50,000, plus costs, plus deleting the articles online – less money, but this time with no confidentiality clause. Towke accepted.

There are, I've been told, some local party members who still vote informally at elections because they cannot bring themselves to vote for Morrison – but nobody has produced evidence of his direct knowledge of or involvement in the campaign to oust Towke and Morrison has denied any knowledge of race being used.

It remains a remarkable fact that, in three of the most significant political moments of his life – Towke's removal, Abbott's removal and Turnbull's removal – Scott Morrison says he had no involvement at all.

———

Morrison, it is said, wanted to represent the seat of Mitchell before he decided he wanted Cook. He didn't have the numbers there either, but it is lucky for Morrison that he failed – Mitchell, in northern Sydney, has no beaches; Captain Cook did not land there; there have not been racist riots there.

When Morrison was asked, a few months after the fact, about the funerals controversy, he said he had been expressing the anger expressed to him by two pensioners who had come to talk to him in the Cronulla mall.

In 2014, he told his local paper that he received 'enormous support' in the Shire over his asylum seeker policies:

I get so much encouragement when I walk through Cronulla mall, go down the beach, or up to Miranda Fair . . . On Australia Day we were at the fireworks at Cronulla and I was walking through the crowd and people were coming up to me to say 'g'day' and encourage me and congratulate me on what we had done so far, and basically saying 'keep giving it to 'em and don't back down'.

The *Leader* reported: 'Asked if there were occasions when he received the "cold shoulder" or stony looks he replied, "not in the shire".'

A TIME

VICTORY

Abbey walked onto the stage first. Really, she marched, and she did it perfectly. She looked straight ahead, then turned her head and looked at the crowd, beaming, still marching. Then she stopped and faced the crowd head-on, still beaming; her movements were precise, like those of a drum majorette. At that point she realised the rest of her family were a little slower, and walked back a couple of steps, the way any child would – she was only eleven. Next came her sister, nine, holding her father's hand. Jen was last, and just as happy as the others. Emerging onstage from a staircase below, she spotted somebody she knew in the crowd; her face lit up and she waved wildly.

In footage of the occasion, Scott Morrison himself appears particularly surprised. He is smiling, but looks as though his comprehension of the world has not yet quite managed to accommodate this turn of events. He has been telling journalists for some time that he believes he can win, but looking at his eyes as he crosses the stage, you sense that this belief was, if not just a line, certainly not much more than skin-deep, perhaps a probabilistic understanding that victory was technically possible.

The prime minister reaches to his inside jacket pocket. His arm goes under his blue tie. Once he has pulled his speech out, he realises he has disturbed the placement of the tie and smooths it down. The crowd begins again the chant that was interrupted – by cheering – when Abbey and the rest of the family appeared: 'ScoMo, ScoMo. . .' This is appropriate: it is ScoMo who has won the election. But it is Scott Morrison himself who looks happy, as though he is beginning to accept the situation as a source of genuine joy, not just shock. He begins to speak. For a moment he is all business as he quietens the crowd and tells them what they already know, that he has received a call conceding the election from his opponent. Then he begins his speech proper.

'I have always believed in miracles.'

He says it seriously, with a serious expression on his face; and then, at the end of the sentence, he smiles. The crowd whoops. And now his happiness reaches a new level; it is as though, in saying those words, relief has hit Scott Morrison. He looks around the room. His teeth are showing. Jenny's face fills with a similar expression. He looks dizzy. And then he becomes the man he usually is in public: a man of confected banalities delivered with a solid faith in the fact that the words he is delivering are impermeable, the types of things somebody like him would say. For a few moments it's possible to believe that you are seeing somebody real; and then he vanishes and is replaced by ScoMo.

———

Australians don't change governments often. When we do, there is a frisson in the air. The 2019 election was not like that. It was boring and nobody seemed interested. It felt like a status quo election. Seasoned hacks and journalists both put their doubts aside and followed the polls – but the election went to Morrison.

Morrison campaigned against change. In his final interview with the ABC before the vote, he described 'Mr Shorten's campaign to change the direction of Australia'. A pollster, Peter Lewis, wrote just before the vote: 'Living in one of the most affluent nations on earth at the wealthiest time in human history, are we, as a nation, happy to just keep staring into our devices and maintain the status quo?' Morrison's campaign was built around this hope. He didn't upset anyone. He achieved this by not doing much at all.

The shortest possible campaign, by law, is thirty-three days. Morrison announced a thirty-eight-day campaign. Easter interrupted, and campaigning was partially suspended, which left thirty days – but after Easter Monday came Anzac Day, on the Friday, which meant many Australians were on holiday that whole week. By the time another working Monday rolled around, just twenty days were left. It was the sort of campaign you chose when you had no policies to talk about.

When Morrison spoke on the first day of the campaign, it was to say two main things. First, that his government would deliver a strong economy. Second, that the election was between two people: 'You vote for me, you'll get me. You vote for Bill Shorten and you'll get Bill Shorten.'

This was the endpoint of the nine-month marketing exercise to which Morrison had devoted himself. It was obvious Liberal research showed that Shorten was a problem for Labor: untrusted, disliked, 'inauthentic'. A potential weakness for Morrison was the fact he was unknown – but every minute of the previous nine months had been spent fixing that problem. The election campaign continued like this, with Morrison calling the numbers at bingo halls and kicking footballs while wearing a baseball cap.

Morrison was presenting leadership as a matter not of belief, but of sensibility, and not of narrative, but of image. He was an ordinary Australian and that was all we needed to know. Everything he had done – most notably the rugby league and the cooking – had been directed at explaining to people that he was a certain sort of person. If they believed this, and liked that sort of person better than they liked the sort of person Bill Shorten was, the sort of Australia he represented, then Morrison might win.

It would be easy to see these as two separate branches of Morrison's campaign: Morrison the suburban dad, and his promise to maintain Australia's affluence by opposing change. Really, they are the same message in different forms. Morrison was comfortable with who he was; Australians, especially those like him, could be comfortable with who they were. Nothing had to change, because there was nothing that needed fixing. We could, in fact, be proud, and keep on doing the admirable things we had already been doing.

The 2019 campaign was, in essence, an extended version of Morrison's 'Where the bloody hell are you?' ad. There had been no specific information provided, no tangible promises. Instead, there had been crisp images that, combined, gave off an aura in place of anything more tangible. Morrison had projected an image of himself and an image of Australia. Even more important than each of these images on their own was the fact they matched each other perfectly.

One of the few interesting things about the 2019 election, apart from its surprise result, was how similar the outcome was to the election three years earlier. In 2016, Malcolm Turnbull had won a bare majority of seventy-six seats out of 150. Turnbull was expected to win, and this near-loss branded him a political failure, which helped ensure his demise. Morrison won seventy-seven seats, just one more than Turnbull. Because he was expected to lose, this made him a hero. It also turned him, in the time it took to count enough of the votes to declare a result, into a political genius.

The most obvious meaning of every election victory is that a political party is given the power to make changes that reflect its view of the world. The second meaning is important too. An election victory – especially an upset victory – establishes, for at least a brief time, the victor as political savant. A type of forcefield is created. If you were right previously when everybody else was wrong, then who are they to criticise your choices? Perhaps you will be proved correct again.

Because Morrison's agenda was so thin, the first consequence of election victories – imposing your philosophy on the world – was not apparent. Rather than rebounding on him, this absence simply served to amplify the second consequence, because it at least provided some definition of the man: here was a supreme player of the political game.

There have long been hints that Morrison himself regards politics as a type of sport. Someone from the NGO sector who had come into contact with Morrison as a minister told me they had the impression that for him, 'behind the scenes it's all a game – we're all just in a game'. In 2018, a Liberal MP told me that, in meetings of

Liberal Party MPs, Scott Morrison loved to use nicknames: 'Lammo', 'Stevie', 'Stuey'. It was, the MP said, like sitting in a football change room. Not long after he became prime minister, Morrison gave a brief interview to rugby league legend Brad Fittler, telling him:

> When I saw Flanno [Sharks coach Shane Flanagan] down when we were doing *The Footy Show* the other day I said, 'Mate, I think I'll take you down to Canberra and let you give the boys a bit of a rev-up about how you play together as one team and stand as one. I mean that's our motto going into this finals series and it's the same for our team. Putting together successive weeks of strong performance, that's what people want to see, [what] they want to see in a football team, they want to see in a government.

Success in most games relies on knowledge and deployment of tactics. A particular level of mastery may demand high creativity – a chess genius, for example, is able to think in ways that other players can't. But a player can become very, very good by rote-learning a set of techniques to be used in certain situations.

Most of all, the idea that Morrison treats politics as a game rings true, because this – rote-learning a set of techniques – is the way Morrison has always approached politics. You can see it in his use, during the 2019 election campaign, of the techniques of the 'Where the bloody hell are you?' ad: the use of images to simplify a concept, to communicate a sensibility, is a crucial aspect of Morrison's approach to the game. You can see it in his repetitive use of phrases, or in the techniques he repeatedly deploys to handle media, or in the consistency of his political battles: the blameless way in which he has benefited from the destruction of Michael Towke, Tony Abbott and Malcolm Turnbull.

Morrison was repeatedly rewarded for treating politics in this manner. He staged a three-ringed circus about strawberries and was applauded – not for doing something, but for the contrived act of looking like he was doing something. He sought to deny refugees health care, and was praised because this was how he would beat Labor. If there were any doubts about the effectiveness of this approach – on either his part or the part of the journalists who joined him in this game – the election swept those doubts away.

––––––

That politicians treat politics as a game is a common slur; I've made it myself. Increasingly, the criticism is made of journalists too, for treating an election as a type of sporting contest. Politics, the critics say, is not a horse race; it affects the lives of millions of people and should be treated as such.

This is a useful critique. It is also naively high-minded. Politics is drama, a battle among humans for power. We have long judged such drama sufficiently fascinating to be the subject of popular entertainment – think *Game of Thrones* – including popular entertainment we now judge to be among the finest art ever produced: *Macbeth*, *King Lear*, *Richard III*. It is both natural and the result of the echo that always runs between art and life that we see actual elections as entertaining too.

There is another reason to ignore the slur. At the heart of politics is a contest: the election. There are nuances here – it is possible to influence policy from opposition – but it is reasonable to say that winning the election is the single most decisive element in politics. It is not unreasonable for a politician who wants to get things done to want to win that election. So it is legitimate, too, that politicians will give priority to winning that election, and filter other decisions through that prism.

Lewis Carroll, author of *Alice's Adventures in Wonderland* and *Through the Looking-Glass*, once wrote the following:

'What a useful thing a pocket-map is!' I remarked.

'That's another thing we've learned from your Nation,' said Mein Herr, 'map-making. But we've carried it much further than you. What do you consider the largest map that would be really useful?'

'About six inches to the mile.'

'Only six inches!' exclaimed Mein Herr. 'We very soon got to six yards to the mile. Then we tried a hundred yards to the mile. And then came the grandest idea of all! We actually made a map of the country, on the scale of a mile to the mile!'

'Have you used it much?' I enquired.

'It has never been spread out, yet,' said Mein Herr: 'the farmers objected: they said it would cover the whole country, and shut out the sunlight! So we now use the country itself, as its own map, and I assure you it does nearly as well.'

There are board games and computer games which seek to replicate some of the strategic calculations demanded by politics, though in a simplified fashion. You could make a game more complex than these games, with each level increasing the amount of information you had to assimilate to make the correct decision – that is, the decision which will help you to win the election. After enough iterations, you would, like Lewis Carroll's mapmaker, end up with the thing itself: politics.

In other words, there is a justification for thinking of politics as a game, which is that politics itself is only an extreme form of the games that are modelled after it. In fact, it is precisely this extremity – the massive amounts of information involved, the infinity of interests to be taken into account – that makes it almost impossible for its practitioners, at least some of the time, to think about it as anything other than a game. To make decisions well, or to make decisions at all, you must find shortcuts through the complexity. Much like following a path picked out for you on a map, these will not be entirely accurate, but they will be useful – that is to say, accurate enough.

Yet the idea of politics as a game feels instinctively wrong, much as when a maths teacher first teaches her students the algebraic trick to show that $0 = 1$. Of course it is just a trick: 0 does not equal 1, and politics is not, ultimately, a game.

The reason comes to us just as instinctively. A game does not, in most cases, have consequences. While we are playing it, we might feel that it does; we might even get very upset when we lose; but unless we have bet a great deal of money on the outcome, we know that the result does not really matter. A game, then, is a type of fiction, a willed and temporary delusion not unlike reading a book or watching a play: while we are playing, we pretend to ourselves that the contest matters, even while we know that it doesn't. This is why we are able to enter the world of a game and then leave it again.

The decisions taken in Parliament House, however, affect us all, in very serious ways. The world of politics is the world itself. We cannot leave it when we want to.

When we say that politicians treat politics like a game, we are not really criticising the fact that they think tactically; we understand this is unavoidable. What we mean is that they have forgotten the ways in which politics is not like a game – they have forgotten that the decisions they make have consequences for those not directly involved in the game. Just as a committed Christian must live simultaneously in a faith frame and a reality frame, a politician must exist in two worlds: the world in which politics is a game and the world in which it is not. The difficulty comes when the former takes over, the outside world vanishes and the game is seen as all.

———

In 1969, *The Selling of the President 1968*, by a young man named Joe McGinniss, spent thirty-one weeks on the *New York Times* bestseller list. Its subject was the successful campaign to elect Richard Nixon, and specifically the television advertising that helped.

It was a sensation largely because what McGinniss unveiled to his readers about the way politics worked seemed strange and new. In the book, an enterprising aide is quoted suggesting live press conferences: 'People will see you daring all, asking and answering questions from reporters, and not simply answering phony "questions" made up by your staff. This would be dynamic; it would be daring.'

The fascination in reading the book now is in seeing the birth of a new political world, however horrible that world has turned out to be (likely even more fascinating because of that horror). McGinniss quotes Roger Ailes, who worked for Nixon and would go on to run Fox News, saying, 'This is the beginning of a whole new concept. This is it. This is the way they'll be elected forevermore. The next guys up will have to be performers.' The campaign consultants were beginning to realise that who Nixon was did not matter; the important thing was who they presented Nixon as being.

Momentous cultural change takes a while to seep into the soil that is a society's common knowledge. Two decades later, the performative aspect of a campaign was no longer new; what was new, at that point, was how thoroughly these rituals had been accepted by political practitioners. Here is Joan Didion describing the campaign to elect Michael Dukakis president: 'Among those who traveled regularly with the campaigns . . . it was taken for granted that these "events" they were covering, and on which they were in fact filing, were not merely meaningless but deliberately so: occasions on which film could be shot and no mistakes made.'

In the same piece, Didion describes the regular occurrence of Dukakis arriving by plane, and then, while waiting to depart, tossing a ball around with his staff so that the cameras could capture the moment:

What we had in the tarmac arrival with ball tossing, then, was an understanding: a repeated moment witnessed by many people, all of whom believed it to be a setup and yet most of whom believed that only an outsider, only someone too 'naïve' to know the rules of the game, would so describe it.

Three decades later, everybody knows the rules of the game. Most senior political reporters in Australia are so tired of this rigmarole that they long ago retired from the campaign trail, and now file their reports from studios, splicing together the predictable footage shot elsewhere. It is only those watching at home (and the junior reporters who must relay the details of such events) who are still tortured in this way.

But none of us is so naive as to take these stunts entirely at face value. At some point, events became detached from their meaning. Once, a candidate throwing a baseball around meant he was throwing a baseball around, and that he was easygoing and ordinary. Later, we learnt to see this in terms of its political intention: the candidate was throwing a baseball around as a publicity stunt, and this meant that he wanted to present himself as easygoing and ordinary. Inevitably, this type of analysis has spread to every aspect of political life, including policy: now everything is analysed in terms of the political strategy being pursued. In other words, politics, or the way we think about it, talk about it and write about it, has become removed from the realm of literal meaning, taking place in an arena in which everything has a hidden meaning.

This was in keeping with the trend of much analysis in the twentieth century, from Freud onwards: a search for the meanings behind things. In psychology, those hidden meanings tend – within the conventions established by Freud – to be found in childhood. When psychiatrists, and later literary theorists, and later still everyone, spoke of hidden intentions, those intentions could be traced back to childhood wishes to sleep with your mother or kill your father (usually both). In politics, those hidden intentions were all traced back to a single narrow desire: the desire to win. In talking about the actions of politicians as a set of gestures that could be deconstructed in order to understand their political strategy, we were talking about politics as a game.

We know it isn't a game. Like politicians, most of us toggle back and forth between these two frames. Also like politicians, we manage to forget, most of the time, our knowledge that it is not a game.

This is because the consequences of treating it as anything other than a game are too demanding. We would have to remember that what is being discussed is, at all times, serious, and often deadly serious. We would have to pay attention to the details, become roused to passion by the topics being discussed. So once we have started acting as though it is a game, it is better to forget the alternative entirely. A reminder that politics is not a game is not only discomfiting but condemning, pointing out that we have been acting trivially – living trivial lives, as trivial people – all this time.

———

There was one small, surprising element in the campaign. An ad produced for Morrison's campaign began with a still photograph of Morrison, Jenny and their daughters. The first bit of actual footage shows the two girls holding a director's clapboard between them – the type of board that is always in shot just before somebody calls: 'Action!' Under 'Production' is scrawled 'Morrison'. The director is listed as Abbey M, and the cameraman is Lily. It is Scene 1, Shot 1, Take 1. The clapboard claps, Lily scrunches up her eyes in a giggle and they both run off.

It is a sweet scene, but also oddly knowing. It acknowledges the artifice of advertising, the knowledge that none of what you are about to see is real. The next scene shows the Morrisons walking together, in a scene obviously contrived for the camera. This should be a fatal tip-off to the disingenuousness of so much of what we are about to see and hear, except that we take that disingenuousness as read: we don't mind this contrivance because Morrison has, in a sense, just winked at us, to make sure we're all in on the joke with him. This is a performance, he is telling us; it is part of the game; you know the rules, and so do I.

FIRES

After the election, Scott Morrison declared that people 'don't want to see politics in their face or anything like that'. In the following months, the government did little. The prime minister said the government was focused only on delivering what it had promised at the election. In July, the government passed tax cuts it had announced before the poll. That same month, when MPs were pushing for a change to Newstart, Morrison told them to be 'mindful of what we took to the election and what we didn't take to the election'. On energy, he said, 'What I took to the election is what I'm going to do.' The government had promised to do almost nothing; it diligently set about keeping this commitment.

In September, four months after the election, and in New York for the United Nations General Assembly Leaders' Week, Morrison was asked about the young climate activist Greta Thunberg. 'She's warning of impending extinction. Her message to you and other leaders is "How dare you?" What's your response?'

Morrison said that climate change was important, but needed to be balanced against the economy. Then he said, 'We've got to caution against raising the anxieties of children in our country. Yeah, we've got to deal with the policy issues, and we've got to take it seriously, but I don't want our children having anxieties about these issues.'

This was impressive diversion: we shouldn't worry too much about climate change because it might make children anxious. The solution, Morrison suggested, was not addressing climate change, but choosing not to make such a big deal out of it.

Attempting to do something on climate change had brought Malcolm Turnbull down, and Morrison was not interested in creating political trouble where there was presently none. There was the added fact that part of his political capital within his party came from his reputation as somebody firmly behind coal. In 2017, displaying his talent for imagery, he brought a lump of coal into the parliament. 'Don't be afraid, don't be scared, it won't hurt you. It's coal,' he said.

At the United Nations, Morrison had said Australia would meet its international climate targets 'in a canter'. Several experts said this was completely false – they would not be met at all – but if they were, Australia would only meet them by exploiting a loophole in a previous agreement that other countries had refused to exploit – what amounted to an accounting fiddle.

In December, environment ministers from around the world met in Madrid for a climate change conference. Australia's exploitation of the loophole was an issue. Morrison's government was determined that the loophole remain in place. An architect of the Paris climate agreement said that Australia was 'just cheating'. Some said Australia was one of the few countries responsible for derailing the talks. The director of one climate think tank said, 'This is a disastrous, profoundly distressing outcome – the worst I have ever seen.'

———

On a Friday in mid-December, the Madrid climate change conference concluded. By then, bushfires in Australia had been burning for months. In some areas they were getting worse. They were attracting massive national and international attention. That day, some areas around Perth were evacuated, while other residents were told it was too late to leave. Over 100 fires were burning in New South Wales.

On Saturday, the prime minister had a night out at a Tina Arena concert, which you could read about on his Facebook page: 'Date night with Jen last night at the new Coliseum Theatre in western Sydney. Great concert, great venue. Congrats to everyone who made it a reality at Rooty Hill.'

On Monday, a Greens MP said he had heard rumours that the prime minister was in Hawaii – but journalists didn't seem to know this, which was unusual. The media didn't even know he was on leave until the Greens MP confirmed it with the acting prime minister's office. Most journalists dismissed the Hawaii rumour as just that, encouraged by Morrison's office, which told journalists it was 'wrong' that Morrison was on holiday in Hawaii – but would not say where he was or how long he would be away.

The next day, the acting prime minister, Michael McCormack, held a press conference and would not say whether Morrison was in Australia.

The day after that, journalist Samantha Maiden reported a source saying, 'ScoMo was checked in to the Jetstar flight to Honolulu a few days ago. He travelled Jetstar business class' – but the Prime Minister's Office would not comment. That day had been Australia's hottest day on record.

The next day was hotter still. A photo emerged of Morrison in Hawaii, wearing board shorts and doing the 'hang loose' gesture with some Australian tourists. Rumours of the prime minister's secret holiday had, by now, become national news. The photo meant they could no longer be ignored or denied.

That night, a tree fell into the path of a truck carrying volunteer firefighters. The truck rolled. Geoffrey Keaton and Andrew O'Dwyer – both in their thirties, each a father with a young child at home – were killed.

Morrison announced he would return from Hawaii early. In a statement he expressed deep regret for any offence caused by his absence. In an echo of earlier radio monologues, when he had focused to a surprising degree on himself, Morrison told 2GB radio: 'I know Australians understand this and they'll be pleased I'm coming back, I'm sure . . . I know that Australians would want me back at this time out of these fatalities. So I'll happily come back and do that.' In between those two sentences, he dismissed any suggestion he had a job to do: 'They know that, you know, I don't hold a hose, mate, and I don't sit in a control room.'

It was a remarkably clumsy performance from a man so recently lauded for his skill in playing the political game. Leaving Australia, its cities blanketed in smoke, to spend time on a beach overseas suggested that he was aloof from the country he led. Keeping it a secret was worse still. That his office had lied about it looked arrogant and ugly. The excuses Morrison offered, his apparent inability to comprehend the reasons for the anger of his citizens, were strange, and suggested an idea that was new to many: that he might not understand the country as well as his victory had suggested. Or, if he did, that he did not understand what was expected of a leader.

———

On the final day of Australia's hottest year on record, thousands of people in Mallacoota, Victoria, fled their town for the lake or beach. At some point they got in the water. By 1.30 p.m. there was fire at the shoreline. Pictures taken that day show people huddled beneath a sky of red (everything in the pictures is red).

In the New South Wales town of Rosedale, the 200 residents left for their beach. They were joined by thousands of people from surrounding areas. Seventeen-year-old Madeleine Kelly told *The Guardian*:

> Flying embers were coming from the ocean, which shows you how it was whipping around us . . . It was almost like you were in the eye of a tornado. The wind was going in circles. Then the fire came over the ridges and we were surrounded by fire. There were five-year-olds on the beach just screaming, they had no clue what was going on. There were newborns strapped to chests. It was just horrible on the beach.

The fires that for many months burned their way across the land were not more lethal than all previous fires, nor did they take over more of the country – but they were more lethal than most, more widespread than most, and they affected many Australians in ways that previous fires largely had not. Many grew accustomed to ash falling on clothes and skin; to a dry throat hurting from smoke; to days spent under a grey sky marked by a red sun. When the fires were over, thirty-four people had died, along with several billion animals.

Another area filled with fire on New Year's Eve was Cobargo, in the Bega Valley. Two days later, knowing he needed to atone, Morrison arrived. Cameras trailing, he walked up to a woman with her hands by her side and said, 'How are you?' She kept her arms where they were. The prime minister reached down, grabbed one arm and shook it, as though it were a malfunctioning electronic device. As he did so, she began speaking: 'I'm only shaking your hand if you give more funding to our RFS [Rural Fire Service]. So many people here have lost their homes.' He patted her lightly on the back as she talked. Another man with Morrison began talking at her and Morrison walked away. Louder, she said, 'We need more help,' but by then Morrison was talking to somebody else.

The clip has been played and replayed on Australian television. Watching it again, it is still surprising: this woman in distress, the prime minister walking away from her. The incident made clear the purpose of the prime minister's visit. It was a photo shoot, nothing more, and when it stopped being a photo shoot he walked onwards to try to return it to its original purpose. The truth is that hundreds of events are manufactured for a politician every year; they *are* photo shoots. What is remarkable about such challenges from citizens – which every politician has experienced – is that they suddenly join the various roles of a politician together: the role of presenting an image to the millions of citizens who will never meet you; the role of governing, which involves listening to problems and responding; and the role each of us must play, of a person among other persons. The striking thing about the hand-shake incident is that, of these three roles, Morrison fulfils only the first, and there seems barely a fraction of a second when he might make another choice.

If Morrison had done this only once, you might dismiss it as a by-product of the pressure he was facing and the tragic situation into which he had arrived. Later that day, Morrison approached a firefighter who was sitting in what looked like a community hall. The man said, 'I don't really want to shake your hand.' Morrison moved his hand to the man's left hand and grabbed it, appearing to move it slightly, then walked on to the next person.

The anger directed at Morrison came in part from a sense that he had never taken the fires seriously enough, and that he'd been slow to act, a sense which the Hawaii farce had then enlarged. A factor in this was his refusal to talk frankly about climate change. In November, a group of former fire service chiefs had met. They used their authority to say that climate change was making bush-fires more intense and more dangerous. They also said that they had been trying to meet with the government since April, to warn of the likely extremity of the coming fire season. The chiefs wanted two things: more action on climate change and more resources for firefighters. By the time Morrison left for Hawaii, they had neither.

Two days after the first disastrous handshake, Morrison announced a series of measures responding to the fires, including the use of the defence forces. A few hours later, a video appeared on social media promoting this announcement. Set to upbeat music, it included pictures of reservists, military vehicles and fire-fighters. It was a political ad, and ended, as all political ads must, with an authorisation: 'Authorised by S. Morrison, Liberal Party, Canberra.'

In response to criticism, Morrison said it was important to communicate to the public what was being done – and then he used a line that sounded a lot like what he'd said at the United Nations when asked about climate change: 'over-analysis of these things can create unnecessary anxiety'. The problem wasn't that he had failed to act at a moment of crisis, or that he had sought to make political capital out of his decision to finally act, but that everybody else had insisted on talking about these things. The facts didn't have to matter, as long as we all agreed not to focus on them too much.

––––––––

Most of the time, the people who harbour the delusion that politics is only a game are hard to spot. Because politics has the form of a game, all its practitioners treat it that way some of the time. Someone who has forgotten it is not a game will, on most occasions, act identically to their colleagues.

Morrison's immense skill at the game should have helped him – except that the game, as he had become accustomed to playing it, had broken down. He was used to following certain rules: if things go wrong, express regret and share the blame around; distract from criticism by making your own announcement; make an ad; do a photo op; shake hands. These worked well within the confines of the game. Now, though, the whole country was either anxious or angry. Genuine suffering was on display. Images, in which Morrison placed so much stock, were now working against him, illustrating something real and unavoidable rather than something trivial and comforting. The separation of the game from reality was impossible to maintain. Faced with the world as it was, rather than the proxy-world his formulas allowed him to handle, Morrison struggled.

If this had simply revealed Morrison's usual approach, it would not have been such a political disaster. But in a moment of crisis, he could not lift, could not find another register – instead, he resorted to the same old tricks. That he treated politics as a game on occasion would have been forgivable, easily brushed past. What the bushfires made visible was that he was incapable of understanding it as anything other than a game.

Morrison made an additional mistake: he made this too obvious. He made the metaphor literal.

Already, in late November, Morrison had attracted criticism for tweeting, tritely: 'Going to be a great summer of cricket, and for our firefighters and fire-impacted communities, I'm sure our boys will give them something to cheer for.'

On New Year's Day, he hosted the traditional gathering for Test cricketers at Kirribilli House; he played a game of backyard cricket. He said the fires and the firefighting would happen against the backdrop of the Test match. 'But at the same time Australians will be gathered – whether it's at the SCG or around television sets all around the country – and they'll be inspired by the great feats of our cricketers from both sides of the Tasman . . .'

Morrison was sharply criticised for implying that the cricket could possibly take people's minds off the fires. The real criticism, though, lay just behind this one. In suggesting that people focus on the cricket rather than the fires, Morrison had displayed, far too overtly, his belief that a game might be made to take precedence over the world itself. He had taken what had been only suspicion and made it conclusion.

As one tweet (from a sports reporter, no less) had it at the time: 'Seriously?! Who is advising this bloke that while the country burns it would be a good look for him to take a photo with blokes who play a GAME!!! YOU SHOULD NOT HAVE TIME FOR THIS RIGHT NOW.'

―――――

Finally, Morrison found a way to turn the game in his favour.

That fire season, two conspiracy theories had been widely circulated, often together: that the two main causes of the fires were arson and the refusal of green activists to allow the preventative burning of areas in the bush (known as 'hazard reduction' or 'fuel reduction'). They were spread by right-wing media figures as a way to argue that the fires were not connected to climate change in any way.

As with most conspiracy theories, these were built atop tiny grains of truth. Arson is always a factor in widespread fires – but what was important about this season was the extremity of the fires, which was the result of intense and unremitting weather conditions. The 'hazard burning' conspiracy had even less substance. Hazard burning had been widely carried out. To the extent that it hadn't, a major cause was the dangerous conditions, the extreme heat Australia faced that year. Even if hazard burning had been carried out in every area, there was a good chance it would not have made much difference: the chief of the New South Wales Rural

Fire Service, Shane Fitzsimmons, said, 'When you're running fires under severe, extreme or worse conditions, hazard reduction has very little effect at all on fire spread.'

These conspiracy theories had been routinely called out. Earlier in November, when the former fire service chiefs held their meeting and announced that the government had refused to meet with them, Greg Mullins, who had led Fire and Rescue New South Wales, said:

This government fundamentally doesn't like talking about climate change. We would like the doors to be open to the current chiefs, and allow them to utter the words 'climate change'. They are not allowed to at the moment. The Grenfell fire in London, people talked about the cause from day one. Train crashes they talk from day one. And it is OK to say it is an arsonist's fault, or pretend that the greenies are stopping hazard reduction burning, which is simply not true. But you are not allowed to talk about climate change. Well, we are, because we know what is happening.

Morrison was not interested – or chose not to listen. In early January, he began repeating the conspiracy theories. Like so much Morrison does, this was only the latest deployment of a tactic that had already worked for him. During the election campaign, he had kicked along the false social media theory that Labor would introduce a 'death tax', alluding to it in his own media appearances. Because the theory was already out there, it did not take much to push it further.

Now Morrison did the same thing. On 4 January, he said, 'As is often the case, those who on one hand say they are seeking those actions on climate change, which we're delivering, can on the same hand, also be those who don't share the same urgency of dealing with hazard reduction.' In other words, the Greens were blocking hazard reduction. The next day he said, 'We also know there have been many occasions where the hazard reduction has been actively resisted.' This could not have been an accident: at that same press conference, he kicked along the arson theory, mentioning 'the number of arsonists we have seen through this fire season'.

When Morrison's usual game-playing failed him, the option was open to him to turn away from the game and acknowledge reality. Instead, he embraced the game more fervently. He spotted a game that others were playing – the spread of disinformation via memes, bots and conservative media – and joined it. Rather than returning to the world as it was, he helped create a new, fictional world, and invited others to join him there.

In late March 2020, *The Australian* reported Newspoll's latest findings. Voters had been asked what they believed the main cause of the fires' severity had been. A majority of those polled – 56 per cent – selected a failure to carry out adequate hazard reduction.

VIRUS

For Australia Day 2020, Scott Morrison released a video. With the fires still burning, he said that adapting to the many challenges of living in Australia was part of our story – and that we would have it no other way. 'We are a people, as Australians, who prevail,' he said, and raised his voice, 'not through luck, or chance, or fortune, but by the efforts and intellect and willingness and determination to stand one with each other.'

The day before, Australia's chief medical officer, Dr Brendan Murphy, had confirmed the country's first case of the novel coronavirus. The patient had been placed in isolation in a hospital in Melbourne, and the process of tracing his contacts had begun. Anyone travelling from the Hubei province in China would be met as they left their plane and advised to seek medical help if they began feeling ill. Murphy said, 'There is at this stage no risk to the general Australian community. And I want to emphasise that.'

Three days later, Morrison announced that his government would evacuate some Australians from Wuhan. They would be flown to the Christmas Island detention centre to quarantine. Two days after that, Morrison announced that anybody travelling from or through mainland China would not be allowed into Australia at all unless they were a citizen or resident.

There was a pause – then, at the end of February, the action picked up again. Morrison said the virus would turn into a pandemic. Travellers from Iran were barred. An Australian who had been aboard a cruise ship, the *Diamond Princess*, died from coronavirus – the first Australian victim. The global death toll hit 1000. Several more Australians died from the virus. Travellers from South Korea were barred, then travellers from Italy. Morrison announced almost $20 billion in economic stimulus.

A few days after that, on a Friday in mid-March, Morrison announced that gatherings of more than 500 people would be banned – but then complicated matters by saying he would still be going to the rugby league that weekend, given the ban did not take effect until Monday. A state president of the Australian Medical Association posted to social media: 'You want to go to the footy? I want my colleagues to stay alive . . . This is not a game.' A few hours later, a spokesperson told journalists Morrison would not attend.

Five days later, Morrison announced that Australians were advised not to travel at all. Indoor gatherings of more than 100 were banned. In the week that followed, all non-residents were barred from entering the country; the first lockdown was announced, along with a second stimulus package, worth $66 billion.

The number of infections was doubling every three days. Mandatory hotel quarantine was introduced for those returning to the country. Fines were introduced to enforce lockdowns. Western Australia closed its borders to the rest of the country. A third stimulus package was announced, of a staggering size: $130 billion.

Infections began to fall. By early May it seemed the virus had been overcome. Seven thousand Australians had been infected, but the daily count of new cases had fallen to around twenty. Morrison told the country it was on the road back. Asked whether there might be U-turns – if we might not have to pause at times, even retreat – he said it was 'like the emu and the kangaroo' on the Australian coat of arms. They 'go forward, not backwards. And that's . . . how this has to work.'

This was a simple story with an aura of blithe optimism. Again and again, Morrison refused to acknowledge potential problems. Early in the pandemic he likened the virus to a 'bad flu'. He did not want to publicly contemplate recession, and warned against using the word 'lockdown'.

Simple stories have their place in politics. Morrison was offering hope. He was encouraging his citizens to be brave and to have faith in their government, and in the future. These are not easy things to do, and up to a point they are admirable. But it is hard to ignore the patronising note in all of it – partly because it has been there since the early days of Morrison's prime ministership.

He delivered his first speech in Albury, from handwritten notes, using a handheld microphone. It was described by several journalists as preacher-like, in an allusion to his evangelical faith. To me, he seemed more like a kindergarten teacher. He gestured constantly: 'I've come to talk to you today about what's in here [points to his heart]. I don't think that, for someone to get ahead in life, you've got to pull others down [arm held straight out, palm angled down and slightly cupped, then swept downwards]. I believe that we should be trying to lift everybody up at once [bends his knees a little and then raises his hand, palm up].'

One of his favourite Question Time routines, early on, was asking his MPs to put their hands up, like schoolchildren. Most did, but some seemed too embarrassed.

A similar attitude was obvious in his language. In that first speech, he delivered the singsong 'Who loves Australia? Everyone. We all love Australia. Of course we do. But do we love all Australians? That's a different question, isn't it? Do we love all Australians? We've got to.' Then there was his apparent belief that it was possible to govern without creating conflict – statements like 'Why do you have to tax people more to tax others less? That's not how you bring Australians together.' He did not seem to recognise that people's interests might run against each other – that creating winners could mean creating losers too: 'We want to see women rise. But we don't want to see women rise only on the basis of others doing worse.' Asked about Labor's plan for companies to publish the pay gap between men and women, Morrison said he would take a closer look, but 'I want policies that bring Australians together, I don't want to create tensions and anger and anxiety in the workplace'.

At some point optimism shades into wilful denial of the facts. In the case of the pandemic, we know that Morrison's various protestations were exactly this. Covid-19 was not at all like a bad flu. The country did fall into recession. Most significantly, the country did retreat into lockdown – again and again. Repeatedly, Morrison's simple stories were proved untrue. He kept on telling them regardless.

———

Writing this from lockdown in Sydney, with the pandemic still 'raging', as the prime minister likes to say, I have trouble summoning up the mood of those early days. The pandemic felt different then.

It is important to try to remember, though, because it gives some sense of the difficulties faced by our leaders. Those early days were chaotic and bewildering. I was in Switzerland, for my partner's work, when the virus began to be taken seriously. We sat at a bar with her colleagues and discussed whether we should leave. We weren't sure, but said to each other that there was certainly no way Australia would stop its citizens from returning.

Within days we had flown back to London, where we were living; and then to Australia. In Singapore our temperatures were checked before we were able to enter the airport's public areas. When we arrived back we self-isolated, and friends delivered groceries. We tried to relax but it was largely impossible. We watched press conferences and checked Twitter.

There was plenty of criticism of Morrison in those early days. He began to deliver long, confusing monologues at his press conferences. In hindsight, this seems minor, and probably unavoidable. Complicated decisions were being taken in a situation unlike anything those involved had dealt with before. Reams of information had to be communicated to a public that was completely inexperienced in such matters; that information was set against the information that was coming in from around the world. The prime minister and the premiers and chief ministers were facing an extraordinarily difficult circumstance.

So it is understandable that, while each individual simple story Morrison told turned out to be wrong, this did not matter much through most of 2020, because a larger, simpler story overtook them: Australia avoided the worst impacts of the virus. As many other nations faced rapidly rising case numbers and astonishing numbers of deaths, Australia kept infections low.

———

Political journalists are much like sports journalists: they love a comeback tale. It is a structural requirement of the political cycle. A journalist can never give up on a politician because anything might happen. This means they must find ways to keep an individual's political hopes alive. This involves constructing seesawing narratives, in which political leaders are up, then down, then up, then down.

Morrison's polling numbers now soared. The story told to explain this was that Morrison had learned from his experience with the bushfires. Many went further: Morrison was close to unbeatable at the next election. Some didn't even hedge their bets.

This prediction relied on the orthodox tale around Australia's response to the virus. That tale ran like this: Australia succeeded. It did this because it acted quickly. The nation closed its borders and instituted lockdowns. Our politicians relied on experts, taking the advice of epidemiologists and medical bureaucrats. Our federal government delivered enormous financial stimulus to the economy. Together, these actions achieved success, limiting infections and restricting economic damage.

Many aspects of these conventional narratives – or at least their connection to Morrison – were questionable. Did Australia act quickly? Scott Morrison's earliest, largest action, the one for which he is still given credit, was to shut the border to travellers from China.

This has been presented, by Morrison's government, as a display of remarkable foresight. In fact, forty nations did the same at around the same time, including the United States and Italy, both of which suffered disastrously from the virus. Shutting the border was useful, but would not have been decisive on its own. For several weeks following that decision, the Australian government did not do very much.

Lockdowns were almost certainly essential to Australia's success – but Morrison tended to hold out against them. The premiers and chief ministers moved ahead of him in the severity of their lockdowns, despite his wishes, and Morrison was quick to criticise the Labor premiers when they did so.

The government did spend a massive amount of money, and significant aspects of the stimulus were well designed – but Australia's stimulus, while large, was not unique. JobKeeper, which was central to the country's economic survival, was just one of many similar schemes around the world. The single most important indicator of whether a nation's economy has done well through Covid seems to be its success in containing the pandemic.

What, then, contained the pandemic? A combination of factors, of course. But there are at least two which are often overlooked in our eagerness for the simpler tale.

The first is that Australia is an island. Being an island did not guarantee success: the United Kingdom, which was accustomed to maintaining travel with close neighbours, failed. But among the nations that did well in the early phase of the pandemic, islands featured prominently: Taiwan, Japan, New Zealand, Cyprus, Iceland, Sri Lanka.

Having a population under 10 million was also a significant

advantage. Australia's population is larger than that, but as the Lowy Institute think tank noted, the nation's federal structure meant its response was best understood as multiple separate responses by different micro-nations, 'a federation of states treating internal borders as if they were international ones', which nations with a smaller landmass could not have managed.

Luck was not the only reason for Australia's early success – but it was a very, very large part of the reason, much larger than is generally accepted. The most interesting fact, then, might be the seemingly eternal prescience of the words of Donald Horne: 'Australia is a lucky country run mainly by second-rate people who share its luck.' We maintain this second-rateness by continuing to believe that it was not luck that saved us, but skill. As Morrison said on the day after the first case of the virus was recorded in Australia, 'We are a people, as Australians, who prevail – not through luck, or chance, or fortune, but by the efforts and intellect and willingness and determination to stand one with each other.'

By constructing a tale about the resurgence of the prime minister, a man who had learned from his mistakes, commentators were not only praising Scott Morrison. They were, unintentionally, imitating him: burying the role of luck in order to glorify the nation, and with it the man who led it and reflected it. Australians, through skill and perseverance, had overcome adversity again.

But what was it, precisely, that Morrison had learned? He had talked down the bushfires – there had been fires like this before – and he tended to minimise the virus and its impacts.

Did he take responsibility? On the economy, he did, but in most other matters – including hotel quarantine, which at various times became a focus of fevered debate – the states took on the bulk of the work and made their own decisions. There was one specific area of federal responsibility – aged care – and there, the government did dreadfully. The Royal Commission into aged care heard that there had been no federal plan to deal with the virus in aged-care homes. Morrison denied this, and pointed the finger at Victoria. This finger-pointing was fair in part – Victoria's Labor government had made a mess of things, letting the virus loose – but it seemed clear, too, that Morrison's government had not acted fast enough to protect the one group of citizens for which it had primary responsibility. 655 people died. Eventually, Morrison apologised.

There was one way in which Morrison seemed to take on more responsibility. This was the creation of National Cabinet, a replacement for COAG, the decision-making body that brought Morrison together with the Premiers and Chief Ministers of the states and territories.

There were three fundamental differences between COAG and National Cabinet. One was speed: National Cabinet could act faster. This was partly because it met more often – this was important – and partly because of the second difference: it was less accountable, and more secret. The government asserted it was covered by cabinet confidentiality, meaning the public had far less access to its decisions or processes than previously (a legal challenge to this succeeded, after which the government began working to pass legislation to restore the secrecy).

The third difference was the most significant. As Griffith University principal research fellow Jennifer Menzies told journalist Amber Schultz in one of the few detailed examinations of the body, she believed the National Cabinet was created for 'rhetorical purposes . . . It got people to understand everyone was working together in the national interest.' In other words, it was an aesthetic change. Morrison had not learned how to be a better leader; but he had learned how to look more like one.

There is an argument, not an entirely unreasonable one, that this is an important aspect of leadership. A leader should not only lead; they must appear to be leading. The argument against Morrison's achievements is not that looking like a leader is unimportant; it is that he has rarely done more than that.

The most notable fact about National Cabinet, as the pandemic wore on, was how much the states simply did what they wanted, and how effective this approach turned out to be. The micro-nations had prevailed.

For quite some time, these were only minor objections to the plot, flaws that did little to puncture the dominant story. If politics were precisely like a novel, this story might have stayed in place, because an author of fiction has the luxury of determining the point at which events conclude. She commits the tale to paper, puts the ending where she likes and is done with it. For the rest of us, our stories continue whether we want them to or not.

It is impossible to say what the final story told about Australia's experience with the virus will be. But we know enough to say this much: in May 2020, Morrison declared that Australia's experience with the virus was coming to an end. We would go forwards, not backwards; we were like the emu and the kangaroo. He was wrong – everything was still to change. This meant the story that had been told about Australia and its success would have to change as well.

DIVISION

When Scott Morrison declared on election night that he believed in miracles, he meant the phrase literally. Two years later, he told a story about the final weeks of the 2019 campaign – a tough time, he said. He had to wait somewhere before speaking at a rally, and so visited a small regional gallery.

> I must admit I was saying to myself, you know, 'Lord, where are you? Where are you? I'd like a reminder if that's okay.' And so I walk in, I didn't know I was supposed to be at Ken's gallery, and Ken's a great Christian guy and I walked into his gallery and there right in front of me was the biggest picture of a soaring eagle that I could imagine and of course the verse hit me . . . The message I got that day was, 'Scott, you've got to run to not grow weary. You've got to walk to not grow faint. You've got to spread your wings like an eagle to soar like an eagle.'

There has been at least one other miracle in Morrison's life, and it came, too, at the conclusion of one of the rare periods in Morrison's life marked by obvious difficulty.

Morrison first met his wife, Jenny, when they were twelve. They met again around fourteen, at a Christian youth camp. This time, Morrison took Jenny's number; he promised to call but never did. At sixteen they began dating. At some point he ended the relationship – for two weeks. At twenty-one they married.

After two years of marriage, they began trying to conceive. 'Just before that I had stopped contraception and I thought I was being really clever and not falling pregnant but when we actually started [trying] it wasn't happening,' Jenny has said. Over fourteen years, she went through ten IVF cycles.

Morrison has said:

It was terribly hard, and it was hard watching the person you love go through something, as you were going through it, but also you're more concerned about what she was going through, while dealing with your own stuff about it . . . And it was a long time. It was a really long time.

Asked what it was like when Jenny told him that another cycle had failed, Morrison answered, 'Oh, you know, the floor falls away. And you feel for her.' At some point the Morrisons decided to name each of the children who had not been born. 'And that was really helpful,' he said. 'Because we'd sort of tried to pretend that we hadn't lost children, but with IVF, actually that's what it feels like.'

It is clear, from some restrained statements Morrison has made, that this time was difficult: 'For families going through this dark chapter of their lives, it's all-consuming – spiritually, emotionally, physically and financially. You question everything: God, each other, your priorities, your future – nothing escapes.' Jenny has been even blunter: 'There were some times that were really hard and you lash out and get angry.' She has said that 'Scott was always super busy so I think he filled his life with a lot of business because he really didn't want to think about that at all'. She could, however, see that he was 'sad inside'. She has also said that her husband is 'gorgeous', that he would always tell her that she was enough for him.

In 2012, Morrison told Jane Cadzow, 'Ultimately, we conceived naturally. Who knows how these things happen?'

There are two potential answers to the 'how'. The first is biological. Morrison has referred gratefully to the dedication and skill of fertility surgeons; Jenny has expressed gratitude to specialists who 'saw me to a better health place where I eventually fell pregnant with both girls'. What this meant became clear in late 2019, when Jenny spoke for the first time about suffering from endometriosis. After a decade of trying to conceive, she saw a different doctor; that doctor sent her back to her original doctor, who told her to give up. Two years later, she sought one more opinion. Soon after, she had microsurgery; three weeks after that, she fell pregnant.

The second reason relies on religious belief. Morrison has written: 'Incredibly, Abbey was conceived naturally (and, we think, divinely).' He has said that he is 'not superstitious, but the fact that [my daughter] was born on the seventh of the seventh, 2007, I believe was not an accident. [I believe] that was a message to me about who's in charge.' He has described the girls as 'miracle children'.

Much like the miracle election victory – which followed Morrison's realisation that he had to run to not grow weary – the miracle of his children's birth did not arrive out of the blue. In his maiden speech to parliament, Morrison said that 'after fourteen years of bitter disappointments, God remembered [Jenny's] faithfulness and blessed us with our miracle child, Abbey Rose'.

A feature of the evangelical faith that Morrison professes is, typically, its intimate experience of God: the sense that God is always with you, always listening, concerned with the smallest aspects of your life – willing, for example, to lead you to a picture in a regional art gallery at the precise moment that you need to see it.

Morrison's descriptions of both his election victory and the birth of his children suggest an additional element: that God is not only watching but will directly reward him when the right thing is done. This understanding of God is far removed from the commonplace phrase 'God works in mysterious ways'. The suggestion is that God works in quite obvious and logical ways. Work hard, do as God commands and you will be rewarded.

Implicitly, this carries with it a division of the world. If good things in life come as rewards, the corollary is that bad things in life are, if not punishments, then at least the logical reflection of a lack of correct action. In other words, people can be divided into the deserving and the undeserving.

I very much doubt that Morrison would ever say this, or even admit to himself that he thinks this way – but there are many things we would never articulate that structure our understanding of the world. Very often, they are things we might not understand about ourselves. They are largely invisible to us, and therefore impossible to separate from the way we exist in the world. This is why they have such power.

———

On election night, having declared that he believed in miracles, Morrison said that his government had been working for 'those Australians who have worked hard every day'. They had their dreams and their aspirations, he said:

to get a job, to get an apprenticeship, to start a business, to meet someone amazing. To start a family, to buy a home, to work hard and provide the best you can for your kids. To save [for] your retirement and to ensure that when you're in your retirement, that you can enjoy it because you've worked hard for it.

Then he declared: 'These are the quiet Australians who have won a great victory tonight.'

Morrison's description of these quiet Australians is remarkable for how repetitive its themes are. As journalist Erik Jensen wrote in an essay about the 2019 election, 'the words all mean the same thing'. One phrase is concerned with love ('to meet someone amazing'), another with family ('to start a family'). Every other word is about earning: 'get a job', 'get an apprenticeship', 'start a business', 'buy a home', 'work hard', 'provide the best you can', enjoy your retirement 'because you've worked hard for it'.

Work is central to Morrison's understanding of his own life. Before Abbey was born, Jenny has said, Morrison filled his life with business in order to distract himself from the pain of failed conceptions; after Abbey was conceived, the situation did not change.

'It was ironic that Scott went into politics when I finally fell pregnant naturally,' Jenny has said. When the two children were

still very young, a doctor – who was seeing Jenny to examine a suspect freckle on her leg – diagnosed her with mild depression. She
told *The Daily Telegraph*:

> I found myself at the doctor's going, 'I'm trying to do every-
> thing and I just can't seem to do it all' . . . Scott went into
> politics as soon as my baby was born, so I've had 12 years
> nearly of him not being around and doing that alone and that
> was really hard and, yes, I suffered and didn't know why.

She once recalled that a friend had said to her, at celebrations for
her twenty-fifth wedding anniversary, 'Yeah but hey, you're not
really celebrating twenty-five, you've probably only seen him for
half of that time'. Jenny added, 'Maybe that's the secret to a good
marriage – some distance apart.'

So much of Morrison's conception of the world seems built
around his personal experience. So it is logical that just as he sees
himself as deserving of success and happiness – the result of God's
favour as reward for his wife's faithfulness and his own hard work –
the people in Australia he sees as deserving, to whom God has
delivered victory, are those who share his values.

Of course, providing for family is an important and understandable focus for many people. One does not have to object to this to
recognise the narrowness of Morrison's view – the sense that he is
unable to imagine that not everybody sees the world in this way, or
that the requirements of a leader might be larger than simply facil-
itating the unquestioned desire of every Australian to work hard
and then retire.

Equally, it is true that many ordinary Australians perceive the world largely through the prism of their own experience. That is no slight on them – but none of them is the prime minister.

———

The boast that the prime minister and the government he led was focused on a particular group of Australians soon took on a more sinister tinge.

Not long after the election, Morrison began to talk not only about focusing on a certain group of Australians but about being on their side. This sounds bland – the usual corporate language – until you recall that governments usually like to claim they are governing for everyone, even those who didn't vote for them. Instead, the prime minister told the parliament that his government was 'on the side of all of those who want to have a stronger Australia, a stronger economy, stronger national security, a more secure environment into the future, a secure region'. That, too, was bland – but then Peter Dutton said that 'this government is on the side of Australians who want strong border protection policies'. A senator told parliament that the government was on the side of people 'who want a job'. Another said it was on the side of 'everyday Australians'. Again and again the formulation appeared, several times in Morrison's mouth.

It got worse. In the parliament, the treasurer was asked by one of his MPs to explain how 'the Morrison government is on the side of Australians who quietly chose sound budget management as a key priority for Australia's future'. The attorney-general was asked to tell the House how the government was on 'the side of

Australians who quietly chose policies that strengthen our national security essential to our safety'.

This was the natural conclusion of Morrison's rhetoric. His government was now explicitly saying that it was on the side only of those Australians who had voted for it. If you thought a certain way, voted for a certain party, you would be rewarded.

———

Another Morrison catchphrase is 'If you have a go, you get a go'. This is not some good-faith promise of support for those who make an effort, but an expression of a particular understanding of the way the world works, because, for some people, it really does work that way. Take Morrison. His life has worked out. He became prime minister! He got what he deserved. This is a world in which luck is a minor factor, with skill and perseverance the major ones in any outcome. This cheerily optimistic statement has a brutal flipside: if you didn't get a go, that's on you.

Morrison has been explicit about this; just how radical his phrasing is has been largely overlooked. Unlike many things he says, it was not muddled, nor did he simply slide it into otherwise unremarkable platitudes. He said it just after he became prime minister, to the first meeting of his new ministry. What he said was this: 'We're going to redefine what fairness means in this country. Fairness means a fair go for those who have a go.'

John Howard had often talked about the importance of having a go. He believed it was part of the Australian mindset. But he was always careful to mention 'a fair go' as a distinct aspect of the Australian make-up, and an essential one; 'having a go' was a separate prong. Morrison has gone much further, making the two into one smooth formulation, by saying that a fair go only applies to those who have a go. Morrison says he wishes to *redefine fairness*. Fairness has meant one thing; now, under Morrison, it will mean another.

Morrison has done little and appears to have little policy ambition. Among all the meaningless verbiage, here is a clear statement of intent, rendered in plain language. It is a rewriting of one of the foundations of this country. And unlike most things Morrison has said, he has backed it up with action.

———

The government's stimulus was staggering in its size – but it was not as capacious as it seemed. Some industries were largely excluded from JobKeeper, the generous wage subsidy. Those workers who lost jobs not propped up by government would join the unemployed on JobSeeker, which most of us know as the dole, and which was worth significantly less.

Public universities were excluded from JobKeeper. Many, many artists were excluded. Many migrants, those on temporary visas, now stuck in Australia because of travel difficulties and money, were not eligible for any help at all. Casuals who had not been with their employer for twelve months were not eligible, which had an outsized effect on young people and women. The list read like a roll call of groups an unimaginative critic of the government might predict would be excluded.

The people on whom Morrison chose to spend money were the people Morrison imagined to be most like himself. They were the people who had a go. They were not people who spent their time engaging with ideas or earned their living by questioning conventional wisdom about what it was to be Australian, like artists and academics; they were not foreigners; they were less likely to be young or female. The historian Benedict Anderson once described nations as 'imagined communities'. Morrison, I suspect, has a very limited imagination. The result is that his view of Australia is stuck, always, in his own experience.

There was an additional reason some people received JobKeeper: these were the people more likely to vote Liberal. Why not make it just a little more likely, by providing those people with money? Since the 2019 election, we have learned of several schemes to buy votes in that campaign. There was the 'sports rorts' saga, in which $100 million was divvied up not according to need or even eligibility, but according to which projects would help win the election. There was a similar scandal around regional grants; and then, in 2021, another emerged around car parks. JobKeeper was far grander than this. Buying votes was certainly not its only purpose – and yet it is possible to see it, as with so many of Morrison's decisions, as a natural extension of political tactics, of the treatment of politics as a game to be won.

———

The story about Morrison coming across a picture of an eagle at a decisive moment in the election campaign comes from a speech he delivered in April 2021. Video of the speech – delivered to a gathering of Pentecostal Christians – had become public. Given Morrison's usual reluctance to talk about his religious beliefs, the speech was closely scrutinised.

Mostly, the scrutiny yielded little. For Morrison's critics, there was no smoking gun that proved he had extreme conservative views. In a way, the speech suggested the opposite: that Morrison held no specific stances derived from his religion. In other words, he had been honest in saying that he did not see the Bible as a policy handbook. The speech gave no comfort, either, to anyone who would have liked to use it to argue Morrison had a coherent philosophy of any sort. There were references to thinkers and brief discussions of their ideas – but the experience of the speech was much like that of Morrison's maiden speech, with his collected thoughts about Australia's history: you were left only with a mess of disconnected, contradictory beliefs. The journalist Bernard Keane put it best: the speech 'provides perhaps the best insight into Morrison's core ideology, and in that sense is one of his most important speeches. It deserves to be taken seriously and engaged with. That core ideology is deep confusion.'

It has never seemed likely that Morrison's attraction to religion involved fidelity to particular texts or beliefs. He has several times switched between both churches and denominations. Judith Brett has suggested that the focus, in Jenny and Scott's adulthood, on evangelical Christianity might have come from a desire to reproduce the vibrant religious communities of their youth: 'Could it be that the heart of Morrison's Christian faith is not dogma but the desire to be part of a community and the chance for an enthusiastic singalong?'

This has the ring of truth to it. Morrison is a man filled with certainty, but, on the other hand, seems less certain about the most important elements of all: his own self and the place it might find in the world. He has always been reluctant to state clearly what he believes. He hates to be held to account – almost as though there is some old fear inside him about getting things wrong and being punished. (He has been open about his father's standards, telling Katharine Murphy, 'You knew if you weren't measuring up – he had a way of making sure you knew.') He reacts angrily when challenged, and has trouble imagining his way into other people's lives. There is an emotional logic to his search for a community in which he might feel safe.

It makes sense, then, that his thoughts about community were at the centre of his speech. 'I've always been at a community church,' he said. 'That's where I want to be, and a church that believes in community and creates community.'

There are those who are determined to go looking for Morrison's specific religious beliefs, as though they might hold some hidden key to unlocking the way he sees the world. As with all the other searches for some secret Morrison, this risks missing what is readily available on the surface. The more useful way to think about the effect of Morrison's faith on his political career is to see in it a sensibility. Rather than offering him a doctrine, its elements have structured the way in which he perceives the world.

The first element is an abiding optimism. This is not specific to Pentecostalism. T.M. Luhrmann has written that faith 'is about having trust that the world is good, safe, and beautiful—a world in which justice is triumphant, enemies are thwarted, and you can thrill at the delicate beauty of the day'.

This is closely related to a second element: the sense of certainty that can come from believing that God has you in his hands – that he has a plan, one that is known, has already been decided and is now being carried out. Morrison has said, of Abbey's conception, 'Afterwards, it really increased my faith because, while I was crying out, wondering, "Where are you?", He said, "I am right here and I knew this day was coming."' On *Kitchen Cabinet*, Annabel Crabb said to Morrison, 'So God changed his mind after fourteen years?' Morrison said, as though it were plain and unquestionable fact, 'I don't think he did, I don't think he changed his mind at all.'

The third lies in the tendency towards binaries. Morrison likes to talk about bringing people together; more often, his actions and rhetoric divide the world. There are the quiet Australians – and everyone else. There are those who have a go – and those who don't; those the government sides with – and the rest, who will have to look after themselves. Pentecostalism places emphasis on the battle between God and Satan. As James Boyce has pointed out, it also divides the world into the saved and those who do not believe. These binaries are decisive, and they have tangible results: if you act a certain way, you will be rewarded.

What assuredness these must add up to: a belief that God is carrying out a plan; a belief that you are one of the saved; a belief that the world is fundamentally good and that your enemies will be defeated.

When Morrison speaks, he is speaking to his imagined community of Australians. His role is not to intervene too much in human affairs; God has a plan and we are all following it. His responsibility, then, is to remind us that the world is good, that things will be alright, that good things will come to those who work for them. This is perhaps why it is easy to imagine him as a preacher or a kindergarten teacher, or even as the coach of a football team: the role he plays, of cheering on his congregation, his team, is common to all.

It is no surprise that Morrison struggles to imagine his way into the minds of people who value doubt over blind faith; people who have good reason to question whether the world is as benign as Morrison believes it is; people who know that uncertainty is real, that anything can happen, and that their enemies may win, as they have in the past.

VIOLENCE

In March 2021, Scott Morrison held a strange press conference. He began by talking about dangerous flooding on the east coast, before moving onto the topics consuming politics: sexism, sexual assault and rape.

This was an attempt to rescue what had become a political disaster. For a month Morrison had been hammered over his inaction and his failure to 'get' what women were up against, both in politics and wider society. The previous night, another story had broken: for two years, a small group of male staffers had been sharing videos of sexual behaviour via Facebook. One had filmed himself masturbating onto the desk of a female MP in Parliament House.

Morrison said the events were shameful. He said he was shocked and disgusted, but pointed out that equally despicable events had taken place in other political parties too.

Having passed judgement on the specific incidents, he moved on to broader issues. He said that women had been putting up with this rubbish for their entire lives – as their mothers had, as their grandmothers had. We had been talking about it in Canberra for a month, he said, but they had been living with it for their entire lives.

It sounded as though the prime minister understood something about the experiences of women, and how different they were from the experiences of men. He sounded emotional. He acknowledged that many women felt he had not previously heard them. What he had heard recently, he said, was stories from women who were afraid to walk to their car from the train; women who were overlooked and talked over by men in boardrooms and press conferences and cabinets; women who were marginalised, intimidated, belittled, diminished, objectified.

The cadences were powerful. It was a strong speech. I was watching it at home, on my laptop, with my partner. It felt as though there was an announcement coming. We watched, and waited. But there was nothing. There were lots of words, and they were good words, but without anything substantial being proposed, they felt thin.

It was clear the press gallery felt the same way. Their questions were sharp. Morrison seemed unhappy. A few questions in, Andrew Clennell from Sky News said to Morrison that if there had been an alleged rape in a business and then these more recent events, the boss's job would be in jeopardy – wouldn't it?

Even these journalists who dealt often with Morrison, and were accustomed to his aggressive tone when asked questions he did not like, found what happened next startling.

Morrison replied, 'I will let you editorialise as you like, Andrew, but if anyone in this room wants to offer up the standards in their own workplaces by comparison, I would invite you to do so.'

Clennell suggested that standards in their workplaces were better than in politics.

Morrison, in response, said there was currently a complaint in Clennell's workplace. A woman had been harassed in a toilet. He mentioned glass houses. He said Clennell was free to criticise, and to stand on a pedestal, 'but be careful'.

Prime ministers sometimes lose their temper in public. This was something else. Morrison seemed to be threatening the assembled journalists. Perhaps even worse, his response to criticism had been to use the authority of the prime ministership to make dramatically public what seemed to be a private complaint.

On their own, these moves would have been surprising – but the really jarring element was that this undermined everything he had just said. Instead of understanding that a woman's experience of harassment should be treated as a private matter, one demanding sympathy and sensitivity, he had turned it into a political weapon to be used to defend himself.

Worse still, it turned out that Morrison was wrong: the event that somebody had told him about was not about Clennell's current employer. In fact, it was not about sex at all. It turned out to be about a senior female journalist confronting a younger female journalist about a matter of press gallery politics.

Even this was not the worst element. It soon emerged that the story that Morrison had mangled was, in its original form, about Samantha Maiden, who had broken the Hawaii story and was also one of the journalists whose reporting had triggered the month-long political nightmare Morrison was now experiencing. Morrison had obviously been trying to intimidate Maiden, and by extension anybody else who might criticise him – or, perhaps, report on similar matters.

Morrison had tried to present himself as empathetic, focused on others, doing what he could. His attack on Maiden made clear that he did not understand any of the things he now claimed to understand, beyond the most superficial level. The press conference had been about him, the political situation he was now in, and what he could do to get out of it. If that required exposing one young woman to public scrutiny, and threatening another female journalist, so be it.

———

On 15 February, Maiden, along with Lisa Wilkinson, had reported an account from Brittany Higgins, a woman in her mid-twenties who, having worked for two ministers, had now left politics. Higgins said that another staffer had bought rounds of drinks, before offering to drop her home in a taxi.

> After arriving at the office, Ms Higgins said she remembers sitting on a window ledge that overlooked the Prime Minister's courtyard. She began to feel unwell and lay down on the couch. It was then she woke up to the Liberal staffer having sex with her.
>
> 'All of a sudden he was on top of me and I physically couldn't get him off of me,' she said. 'I woke up mid-rape. I told him to stop. I was crying. He wasn't even looking at me. It felt like I was sort of a body that was there. It didn't feel like it was anything about me.'

That day, in parliament, Morrison was asked about the assault. He said it was deeply distressing, bureaucratically defended his government's actions in responding to the alleged rape – 'best practice' had been followed – and said it was important Higgins was listened to and respected.

The next day he began a press conference by saying that he had spoken to Jenny the night before and that she had said to him, 'You have to think about this as a father first. What would you want to happen if it were our girls?'

Most of what Morrison said at this press conference was reasonable. But much of the commentary afterwards was dominated by criticism of this particular phrase. Not that long ago, it might have gone unremarked. But such suggestions – I care about women because I'm a father, because I have a sister and so on – had come under increasing attack in recent years. Why did Morrison need to talk to his wife before he understood that allegations of a young woman being raped required a much stronger response than a bureaucratic defence of his government's actions?

In an indicator of how much pressure Morrison was under that day, he was asked directly about this attitude:

JOURNALIST: You said this conversation really hit home when you had it with Jenny and thought about it as a husband and a father. Shouldn't you have thought about it as a human being? And what happens if men don't have a wife and children? Would you . . . do they reach the same compassionate conclusion?

PRIME MINISTER: Well, look, in my own experience, being
a husband and a father is central to me, my human being. So
I just can't follow the question you're putting.

This answer attracted less attention, but it is by far the more
remarkable answer of the two, because of how explicitly Morrison
describes the limits of his own imagination. Morrison says, almost
incredibly, that he *can't follow the question*. The reason he can't even
grasp what is being asked is because *being a husband and a father is
central to me*.

This is one of those moments exceedingly rare in Morrison's
career, an actual gaffe: when he accidentally says something revealing
and true. Sometimes, when gaffes occur, the politician instanta-
neously knows; they realise that they have given themselves away. In
those moments, the mask that they are accustomed to wearing literally slips – their 'face falls' – and you see as well as hear the truth.
This is because they have been giving an insincere performance and
have been caught out.

Morrison's performance is entirely sincere. He does not realise
he has been caught out – cannot realise – because he does not even
understand what it might mean, in this situation, to be caught out.
Asked to imagine being somebody other than himself, he says that
he is incapable of it; and then, going further, that he does not even
understand what is being asked. The answer is stunning in its honesty; and it is so honest because Morrison cannot see the problem
with the answer.

———

Three weeks before he threatened Maiden and the rest of the press gallery, Morrison had lost his temper with another journalist. Towards the end of a press conference on the Royal Commission into Aged Care Quality and Safety, Anne Connolly, who had a detailed knowledge of the area, asserted that the government supported a particular recommendation. Morrison, obviously peeved, asked her how she knew that. Connolly, who seemed to know more about the topic than the prime minister, said she knew because the government had already put that position in a submission. Morrison said, 'I'm sorry. The government has made no decisions on the findings of this report. So it's simply incorrect for you to suggest that.'

Connolly tried again: 'The Department of Health and the regulator put a submission in to the royal commission –'

This time, Morrison spoke over her. 'I'm the prime minister. This is my minister. Our cabinet will decide our response to this royal commission, okay? So we've released it. I think I've answered your question. Thank you.'

Watching footage of the exchange is unnerving. Morrison's response implied that the question was not important, and that Connolly, a respected journalist with obvious expertise in the subject matter, was being impertinent, a schoolgirl who had stepped out of line. Morrison delivers this reminder of his authority with a small, tight smile on his face. It is the type of smile that somebody might wear in a heated argument when they think they have come up with an unassailable rebuttal of the other person's case; it suggests a somewhat nasty thrill in his own cleverness, the fact that he can say those words – 'I'm the prime minister' – and Connolly can't.

On at least three separate occasions Morrison has, reportedly, used this phrase to respond to a woman. Julie-Ann Finney's son took his own life after two decades serving with the navy. According to Finney, when she asked Morrison why he wouldn't call a royal commission into veterans' suicides, he said, 'Well, Julie-Ann, I am the prime minister.' As Finney put it, 'That is not a reason.' (Much later, Morrison did call a royal commission.)

Just after Morrison became prime minister, he found out that a Liberal MP, Julia Banks, had decided she would not run at the next election. He asked her to wait before announcing her decision. Banks refused. He made various offers in order to persuade her, but she still refused. Morrison, she said, was getting 'really angry'. Finally, he said, 'Julia, I am the prime minister.' Banks agreed to delay her resignation just twenty-four hours. During that small window, she later said, Morrison's office began telling the press and members of her party that she had had 'a complete sort of emotional breakdown'.

Banks' announcement attracted attention for another reason. She made accusations of bullying and intimidation, both from within her own party and from the Labor Party. Other senior Liberal women were making similar complaints about their own party, specifically about bullying during the leadership contest. Julie Bishop even suggested the bullying may have crossed into illegal behaviour.

Morrison batted these accusations away, saying they were not his priority; then ordered a review. The review was delayed. Two women, former Liberal staffers, came forward to say they had been sexually assaulted by other staffers, but this seemed to do nothing to speed the process up. The final result – a new code of conduct for the party – was criticised by those women for being close to useless.

———

Brittany Higgins' allegations were the beginning of a saga for the Morrison government. There were reports that Morrison's office had been briefing journalists against Higgins' partner – just as Banks said they had briefed against her. There were reports that some members of Morrison's office had known about the alleged rape well before it became public, which raised the question of how the prime minister could not have known. To deal with this, Morrison ordered an inquiry by the head of his own department; the inquiry was suspended twice and has, at the time of writing, still not concluded. Historical rape allegations against the attorney-general, Christian Porter, were revealed; he denied them, and Morrison kept him in the cabinet (though he demoted him from attorney-general, giving other reasons. Six months later, Porter resigned as a minister for another related, though different, reason).

A week before Morrison's threat against the press gallery, protests were held in capital cities and at Parliament House. Tens of thousands of people – mostly women – joined the March4Justice. Morrison chose not to leave Parliament House to greet the protesters (and the organisers of the march refused to come to Parliament House to meet with him). In the House of Representatives that day, asked about this decision, he said similar protests were met with bullets elsewhere, calling such marches in Australia a 'triumph of democracy'.

Morrison was slammed for this comment, which was widely interpreted as suggesting that the women protesting should be grateful they weren't being shot at. This was an unkind interpretation – but the very unkindness was significant, pointing to the intensity of the anger now directed at Morrison. He had said much the same thing before, about other protests – but now his words were heard differently. This was true, too, of his homily about understanding the dangers faced by women through the prism of his daughters – he had said it before, and it had been largely ignored.

It was true of all the tactics he had used to deal with the controversy. All of them had been tried before, and all of them had worked: briefing against those who criticised his government, arguing that fault lay with others, obfuscating about who knew what when, using bureaucratic language to smother an issue, trying to wait the controversy out, returning to stock phrases.

This pattern was familiar from the bushfires. There was no lightbulb moment, no sudden breakthrough into a deeper understanding of why he was failing. Morrison just kept mechanically cycling through tricks he had used in the past, desperately hoping something would work.

———

When reports of bullying against his female MPs surfaced, in 2018, Morrison seemed uninterested. When allegations of a rape just fifty metres from his own office were made, the minister who knew about the allegations did not raise the matter with him or his staff. Rather than facing troubling events, the government seemed to have a habit of turning away.

In the United States, the Black Lives Matters protests sprang up during the pandemic. They were adopted here, because Indigenous Australians have their own experience of violence committed by the state: not only in the original act of violent dispossession, but the appalling mistreatment of Indigenous people by police that goes on still, and which has led to many deaths.

Morrison was asked about the American protests. He said the murder of George Floyd was shocking; also that the looting that followed wouldn't help change anything. He said, 'We have our problems. We have our faults. We have our issues. There's no doubt about that. But when I see things like that, I'm just very thankful for the wonderful country we live in.'

Two days later, in an interview on the same radio station, Morrison said Australia had 'issues in this space'. On Friday, at a press conference, asked if it was a national shame that at least 432 Indigenous people had died in custody since the royal commission on the issue thirty years earlier, he said of course, noting 'the problems we have in this area', 'these issues' and 'these concerns'. His use of neutral language was relentless.

At that same press conference on Friday, he urged people not to attend protests. Expressing fear that the coronavirus might spread, he cited examples of the sacrifices of people who had not been able to visit nursing homes, or attend funerals, and spoke in moving terms about 'those who had the absolute agony of not being able to say goodbye to a loved one'.

Morrison might have used the same words, without a single change, to explain to listeners the grief and rage that drove people to protest while the threat of a pandemic had not entirely vanished.

The hundreds of Indigenous people who have died in cells: their families, too, 'had the absolute agony of not being able to say goodbye to a loved one'. In Morrison's words, across several days, one group of people were allowed their grief; the other had their grief smothered by a blanket of anodyne language that would trouble nobody who was not already upset.

————

Talking in specific terms about death inflicted by the state and then insisting that our country is 'wonderful' might prompt the question: wonderful for whom, exactly?

The belief that Australia is a wonderful country that deserves its success and where things will just keep on getting better is extremely important to Morrison. There is no sentiment he expresses more often. Pain, violence and trauma have the potential to upset this story: to make clear that all is not well. There is another story that they upset, a story of equal importance to Morrison: that politics is a game. Our bodies are the limits of our ability to turn everything around us into a set of harmless fictions, in which politics is merely a very complicated game of strategy. A body that is harmed, that has damage done to it, that has the life taken from it refutes the idea that politics is a game that can be played without consequences.

Most of the time we manage, nonetheless, to suppress these troubling facts – just as Morrison does. He does not want to talk about the Cronulla riots; he uses bland euphemisms to minimise massacres of Indigenous people, as well as more recent violence against them; he has no interest in discussing the cruelty deliberately visited upon refugees in our care. By positioning the victims of such violence as outside the imagined community of Australia, the moral community for which we all have responsibility, we make these victims, and the violence inflicted upon them, disappear.

The fires made physical harm visible and impossible to ignore. The victims were too close to the traditional idea of what it is to be Australian: white, male, from the regions rather than the city. Nobody could pretend they were not part of Australia, or that their pain did not matter. Not long ago, a mass movement of women might have been ignored, at least by many men; but changes in the past decade – the #MeToo movement, a female prime minister – had made that impossible too. Women had claimed a new place in the Australian imagination.

The fires and sexual violence caused the greatest and most sustained shocks of Morrison's prime ministership to that point – because they revealed gigantic cracks in Morrison's worldview. Each said, in effect: Australia is *not* as perfect as you think. It is threatened by climate catastrophe, and the action our government is taking is making that more likely, not less; and one half of our population lives under latent threat of violence from the other half.

———

In her book about violence against women, the cultural critic Jacqueline Rose writes:

Narcissism starts with the belief that the whole world is at your feet, there solely for you to manipulate. Beautifully self-serving, its legacy is potentially fatal – as in the myth of Narcissus, who drowned in his own reflection in a pool –

since it makes it well-nigh impossible for the human subject to see or love anyone other than themselves. Aggressivity is therefore its consequence, as the child struggles with the mother or whoever takes her place against the dawning recognition that they are as helpless as they are dependent on others to survive.

Rose's argument is that male violence is not an indication of strength, but a sign of weakness. The man feels weak and vulnerable; to cover this fact, to assert to himself and to others that he is strong, he lashes out.

This is a fair approximation of what was happening to Morrison in the month or so when his political authority was challenged by the sudden rush into the public space of women's stories. He was being challenged on every one of his favoured grounds. His identity as a political genius was under attack. His conception of politics as a game that could be mastered with a set of repeatable skills was no longer functioning. His personal identity as a husband and a father was turned against him.

Perhaps most disturbing, his political identity was under attack too. His election victory had been achieved largely by establishing himself as the embodiment of a particular version of Australia. That Australia was fair, it was glorious, it was blokey. If Morrison's idea of Australia – the idea that he put forward at every opportunity – was under attack, then so was his political future, because he had staked everything on this idea.

Victory at the election had given Morrison enormous authority, within his party and without. His apparent political recovery during the pandemic reinforced this. There was a sense that he was an unbeatable political force. But as Rose points out, 'No human, however powerful, is spared confrontation with the limits of their own power.'

Morrison had been accustomed to acting as though the whole world was at his feet; he had performed his manipulations brilliantly. What was now happening was beyond his control – even beyond his conception. A politician more able to look outward, to take into account other people, might have been able to open themselves in this moment. Morrison, as usual, struggled to understand the implications beyond himself.

When journalists began to challenge Morrison with their reporting, their columns and their questions, this must have been particularly confronting, because of Morrison's acute understanding of the power of journalists. He relied on them to tell his stories. Now they were resisting. This was the confrontation with the limits of his own power that every powerful person hates.

It is unlikely to be coincidence that many of the journalists who had made the most piercing critiques and asked the most piercing questions of Morrison over the years had been women: Jane Cadzow, Julia Baird, Laura Tingle, Michelle Grattan, Niki Savva, Katharine Murphy, Samantha Maiden. It seems likely they recognised something in Morrison that men, at least at first, struggled to see – or perhaps were blind to, in the way that Morrison himself is blind to so much.

During those months, this more sceptical view began to spread. Many columns made reference to aspects of the prime minister that had been visible for some time – his lack of empathy, his tendency to politically manage situations rather than lead, his unwillingness to take responsibility – but that had never quite gained a foothold in the commentary about him.

When Morrison twice, during this period, lashed out at journalists, there was a distant echo, in his aggression, of the violence he had condemned. Each proceeded from a similar impulse, the struggle against vulnerability and the overwhelming desire to reassert control. When you declare 'I am the prime minister', it is not because you are assured of your standing but because you feel your authority slipping away.

PAST, PRESENT, FUTURE

If Morrison believes in signs from God, winged messengers sent to spur him onwards, does he believe in bad omens too? Warnings from God that he is about to be tested?

Midway through 2021, it was announced that a woman who had been charged with putting needles in strawberries – the act long assumed to have triggered the first 'crisis' of Morrison's prime ministership – would not be tried. The prosecutor was dropping all charges.

Michelle Grattan wrote that this pointed to the comparison between the Morrison of then and the Morrison of now: the action-man image had been seriously damaged.

The very next day, Victoria announced it would enter lockdown. This meant that – because New South Wales was already there – almost half the country was now locked down.

The next week, on FM radio, Morrison was asked if he would apologise for the 'nightmare' vaccine rollout. One host, Jase Hawkins, said, 'I've never heard the word sorry. "Guys, you know what, sorry. We did screw it up, but we're getting it right now."'

Morrison said there had been problems and they had dealt with them and he was accountable.

'Can you just say, "Sorry, Jase"?' the radio host persisted. 'It will make me feel so much better and then I feel like I can move on.'

Morrison repeated his answer again.

Jase told him he would even take a 'my bad'.

Morrison repeated his answer.

Jase tried one more time: 'I've got one for you – what does this spell, S-O-R-R-Y?'

The day after that, obviously pricked by losing the confidence of FM radio hosts and their quiet Australian listeners, Morrison said sorry.

———

Back in August 2020, there had been news of a 'deal' that had been 'inked' on vaccines, a 'guarantee'. The prime minister vigorously promoted the achievement on television and radio – though the 'guarantee' turned out only to be a vaguer letter of intent. A few weeks later, the government announced what was pretty much the same thing, a 'supply and production agreement'. In the next months there were more vaccine announcements, more boasting about what they would deliver to Australia. When Morrison turned up for his own vaccination wearing a green-and-gold T-shirt with 'SCO-MO' emblazoned on the back, and with an Australian-flag mask on his face, it seemed like the beginning of a long series of triumphant photo opportunities that would entrench his identity as the architect of Australia's success.

Instead, the vaccine rollout was a disaster.

In December 2020, the health minister, Greg Hunt, announced that all vaccinations would be completed by October the next year.

In January 2021, another target was set: 4 million jabs by the end of March. Then the government's rhetoric began to shift. Instead of everyone being fully vaccinated by October, everybody would only have had their first dose (of two) by then. The March target was missed – instead of 4 million doses, there had been just over half a million – and then Morrison abandoned targets altogether. By midway through July, Australia was the least vaccinated of the thirty-eight rich nations belonging to the Organisation for Economic Co-operation and Development.

Stephen Duckett, who had once led the federal health department, told the ABC, 'I think our vaccination strategy has been one of the worst in the world.'

When Morrison had been in his vaccination announcement phase, he had proudly declared Australia was at 'the front of the queue'. In March, with the rollout lagging, he began declaring, defensively, that it was 'not a race'.

As public anger grew, Morrison was attacked for this expression. He blamed the chief medical officer for using the phrase first, and declared he had only used the phrase to describe the approvals process for vaccines, which was not true. Finally, in July, not long after the Tokyo Olympics had begun, he admitted he should not have said it, and announced a nationwide 'sprint', in which 'we make a gold medal run all the way to the end of this year'.

———

Australia's failure to vaccinate its population was humiliating because it was awful. It was even more humiliating for how it exposed our national habits. Australians were slow to get vaccinated. We were in no particular hurry – partly encouraged by the prime minister's assurances that it was not a race. Other nations had to rush, but we had time on our side. There was a sense, after the nation's success in 2020, that everything would be fine. Somehow, many Australians managed to ignore the fact that Melbourne had spent half of that apparently glorious year in lockdown. Things had already gone wrong, but we somehow convinced ourselves that the future was inevitably bright – that we had earned it and it would be ours. And then, suddenly, many of us were in lockdown, panicking about not having had our vaccinations. There were lengthy waits now, as people rushed to get vaccinated, and we understood, then, why the government had not wanted to encourage us, had not promoted vaccinations very hard: there were not enough to go around.

As usual, the chief optimist was Scott Morrison. He had declared we could only go forwards not long before Melbourne, in 2020, was plunged into months-long lockdown. In 2021 he repeated the mistake, declaring lockdowns would be a 'last resort' not long before New South Wales went into its long winter lockdown.

For some time, Morrison insisted that the rollout was on track. When this became implausible, he found others to blame. The panel of medical experts advising on vaccines, ATAGI, had given incredibly cautious advice about the use of the AstraZeneca vaccine, which caused blood clots in a tiny fraction of people – advice that was a major factor in the reluctance of many Australians to use one of the vaccines on offer. Morrison also cited Europe's decision to block the shipment of millions of doses to Australia.

These specific problems could not have been foreseen – but this did not absolve Morrison, because the emergence of some problem, somewhere, was guaranteed, especially during a global pandemic. It became clear, with time, that Morrison's government had failed to take the precautions that other rich countries had taken, by investing in a wide enough range of vaccines to ensure that vaccinations could go ahead even when obstacles arose. That Australia seemed to have planned for the best-case scenario, not the worst, was in line with Morrison's blind faith that all would be well.

This was not the only mistake. GPs began to complain about unpredictable, disorganised delivery of vaccines. Twice, Morrison appeared at late-night press conferences to make apparently rushed announcements about AstraZeneca, which increased confusion. News kept emerging of vulnerable groups that had not been given the priority the government had led them to expect, including aged-care workers and people with a disability. By late in the year, vaccination rates for Indigenous Australians were far behind those for other Australians.

The media began to turn on Morrison. The traits which had begun to receive notice during the crisis over sexual violence began attracting more attention still. Voters were clearly frustrated: Newspoll showed Morrison's personal approval ratings, which had been falling fairly steadily since July 2020, continuing to drop. In August 2021, for the first time since the Covid crisis had begun, the Australians who disapproved of the job he was doing outnumbered those who approved.

———

In September, Morrison posted a photo of his family. They were petting a white dove. The caption, to mark Father's Day, read:

Being a Dad is a special gift that we are given in life. It is a great blessing in our lives. On the day this photo was taken of our family together earlier this year I was reminded of just how precious that gift is. To all the Dads, have a great day and never forget how fortunate we are to have the tremendous opportunity to love, cherish and care for our kids.

The suggestion seemed to be that Morrison was posting this old photo because – like some other fathers around the country – he would not be able to see his kids this Father's Day due to Covid restrictions. In truth, Morrison had flown to Sydney that weekend, then back to Canberra. This fact was only confirmed by the Prime Minister's Office after journalists asked.

This had happened before: the weekend before his secret trip to Hawaii, he had done a similar thing, with the photo of him and Jen on 'date night' at Rooty Hill, seeing Tina Arena.

There was a third trip Morrison had tried to keep secret. Midway through 2021, he had travelled to England for a global summit. At the end of the trip, with most Australians unable to travel, he had taken a detour to visit the area where an ancestor, William Roberts, had been born – the Roberts whose suffering on arrival in Australia Morrison had so vividly described on Australia Day in 2019. Again, the public had been kept in the dark; again, Morrison could not see what he might have done wrong.

This pattern might at first seem like Morrison's usual habit of repeating political tricks. What is odd in this case, though, is that he was not repeating a trick that had worked, but one that had failed. Hawaii had been the most damaging event of his prime ministership. Why risk repeating it, in such similar form – secret trips focused on his family in the middle of a crisis – not just once but twice more?

You would think that Morrison's relentless focus on visibility, on voters and on public perceptions of himself, should have prevented these mistakes. Actually, they made them inevitable. A man who allows his public persona to crowd out his private self will never give over to it entirely. The place taken up by his real self might shrink, but in some ways this makes it more important, not less, and makes the task of defending what is left essential. He is like those artists and comedians who, spending so much of their lives on display, must wall off some part of themselves in order to survive. Morrison, in order to protect the most important parts of himself – his family and his religion – imposes a radical separation.

This is precisely what he told Annabel Crabb, and what he told Barrie Cassidy: that there was the minister doing a job, and then there was Scott Morrison.

Leading a nation, though, is not merely a job. It is not a set of tasks that can be neatly separated from the person who does them. If an artist who insists on separating their soul from their work will produce only empty work, the same is true of a prime minister.

There has always been an odd hollowness at the centre of Morrison's prime ministership. We do not know what he believes or what he wants to do. He is often absent, it seems, from decisive events. He is almost never at fault, it seems, when things go wrong. He has, with time, fashioned a government in his own image, one in which secrecy dominates and it is almost impossible to find somebody to answer for their actions.

Many of Morrison's habits were apparent before the 2019 election. We did not let this bother us: we were content to elect a flat character and accept the thin performance that Morrison put on for us.

The years since have demanded something different. It was not possible to do what many of us wanted to do – what Morrison believed we wanted to do – and forget about politics. We were reminded of the ways in which politics matters, and we began to want a leader, too, who understood that politics mattered, and that he was required to bring his whole self to the task.

This is likely to be a century of crisis; perhaps this can be said of every century. In this case, we know what some are likely to be. Prime among them is the climate crisis, which will bring others with it. There is a higher chance of pandemics now. We are also likely to see an intensification of the refugee crisis, as people flee the disastrous effects of climate change in their own nations. The balance of power in the world is changing quickly too.

We already know how Morrison is likely to respond. He will soothe us, as though we are anxious children. He will encourage us to be quiet, urge us to look away, and tell us that these problems are being handled, somewhere out of sight. He will provide other things that we can look at instead: a series of crisp, attractive images that remind us of the wonderful place we live in and that buoy us up with the idea that it will always be the way it is right now.

Perhaps we will remember what we learned these past three years; or perhaps we will do exactly as he suggests, in the hope that we might sleep as soundly as he does.

MORRISON'S AUSTRALIA

For a long time, Christmas Island was most famous for its spectacular migration of red crabs. Late in each year, millions and millions and millions of these brightly coloured crustaceans leave their homes and march across the island to the ocean. David Attenborough once attended, and there is footage of him standing on a clifftop, the spray of the waves behind him, describing 'the savage, rocky shores', where, years later, fifty asylum seekers would die in a wreck.

It was in September 2001, that fateful month, that the island acquired a new, strange notoriety. After the political crisis in which the government would not allow the *Tampa* – carrying refugees its captain had rescued – to dock at the island, Prime Minister Howard arranged for a new law to be passed, excising Christmas Island and other remote territories from Australia's migration zone. If you landed within the zone, you were subject to Australian visa law. If you landed outside the zone, you were not.

At that moment, Christmas Island became two things at once. The Australian government could make laws about it – and one of those laws was that it would not be bound by Australian law. It was Australia and not Australia, both at once.

I was reminded of this in May 2021, when Scott Morrison – whose career was so bound to Christmas Island, first in the funerals controversy, then in the Medevac show and then in the island's use as a quarantine station during the pandemic – banned flights from India from landing in Australia.

Covid-19 had begun spreading rapidly through India. For a brief period, Australian citizens there were stopped from coming home, despite the urgency of the worsening health situation. If they tried, the government said, they faced imprisonment.

This was the natural extension of the caps the government had placed on arrivals from overseas. Already, tens of thousands of Australians wanted to get home but couldn't. Now, for those Australians in India, Scott Morrison had cleaved the rights of citizenship from the status of citizen. Morrison had made a group of Australians both citizens and non-citizens at once.

This approach is embedded in our history. It was there from the moment of the founding of this nation. The land was neither uninhabited nor ownerless – but the assertion that it was allowed the British to claim it. Paradoxically, this claim then provided an imperative for the new arrivals to protect their ownership of the land, including by murdering the people who were already here. It was both empty and not empty at once.

This is the most important fact to understand about our country. We are always splitting ourselves in two, then turning away from the half that troubles us. John Howard did it, when he said that pride must displace shame. Donald Horne did it, when he said that the elites were complacent, but that this had nothing to do with the people. This act – of taking a thing known or very deeply felt about our country and attempting to slice it off – points directly at the reason we do it: if the excised part was not a threat, there would be no need to excise. The truth is that these parts of ourselves are so strong that they threaten to overwhelm the rest, and this is why they need to go.

We have always known that we are a land of extremes – of fire and flood, of rainforest and drought – but these extremes dominate the way we think about ourselves too. We insist that we are extremely this, in the hope that it will drown out the possibility – the likely truth – that we are its opposite. We do not merely refuse to acknowledge the truth of things; we go so far in the opposite direction because it is the only way to maintain our belief in a world so obviously not the one in front of us. We put enormous effort into acting proud because our shame is such a threat. We pretend we are a working-class people, although we are among the richest people in the world. We call ourselves the land of the fair go while managing, for a century or more, to maintain so many of our Indigenous Australians – those with a greater claim to this land than anyone else – in a state of poverty and early death.

Scott Morrison does it too, when he insists he is authentic, not inauthentic, that he is not pretending to be someone he is not, that he is not a phoney.

————

For a while, I thought the aim of this book would be to discover the real Scott Morrison beneath ScoMo. What facts might I turn up that would complicate our picture of him; what new revelations might help us understand him better?

Almost four decades ago, the theorist Eve Sedgwick asked her friend Cindy Patton her opinion of the 'sinister rumours' that the American military had spread AIDS deliberately. Patton responded by saying she wasn't interested one way or the other. What could this possibly tell us? That the government barely cared about gay men and drug users? That 'people in power look calmly on the likelihood of catastrophic environmental and population changes'?

In other words, if the outlandish and horrifying conspiracy theory turned out to be true, 'What would we know then that we don't already know?'

Eventually, I realised that Sedgwick's point applied to questions about who Scott Morrison might really be.

If we managed to confirm, beyond doubt, that Morrison does not care about climate change because he believes we are already in the End Times, what would that tell us that we don't already know? We can tell he has little interest in acting on climate change from how little he has done and from his repeated efforts to derail honest public debate about its impacts.

If the inquiry into who knew what when about the alleged rape of Brittany Higgins was ever concluded, and determined that Morrison's staff had known and had not told him, or even (this is incredibly unlikely) that Morrison had been told, what fresh insight would this furnish? That Morrison's government is secretive and unaccountable, uninterested in events except as political problems to be managed?

By this point in Morrison's prime ministership, a set of recurring traits is clearly visible. There is the dependence on tactics, a sense that politics is a game to be won. There is an overreliance on cheery platitudes in the place of serious thought. There is the inability to see out from his own narrow view of the world, his tendency to focus only on those who remind him of himself, and the defensiveness that arises when he is asked to do otherwise. Most importantly, there is a stubborn, reality-denying belief that everything will turn out well.

If we do not judge Morrison harshly for these things it cannot be because we don't know; it must be either that we don't want to know or that we don't much care.

With time, we have all become incredibly skilled at finding ways not to look at what is in front of us. We do it when we analyse politics in terms of political manoeuvres and techniques, at the expense of focusing on what is actually being done. We are ignoring what is happening in favour of some secret story just behind it, that excuses the thing being done by telling us the politician didn't really mean it, or that's not really who they are.

It is what Morrison does when he explains that Jen did not want him to get the Immigration job, but he took it and did it as well as he could, because 'What should I have done? Not stop the boats? What should I have done? I'm pleased that in the things the prime minister has asked me to do, I've had some success . . .' It was just a job; it was not a reflection of his own beliefs. It was a role that he took on, because that is the way the game of politics is played.

———

The distancing of politics from reality that began its creep sometime in the 1970s and reached what we can only hope is its peak in recent years meant, it is only possible now to see, that it was inevitable we would end up not with politicians who were people, but politicians who were caricatures, made up only of the most obvious, surface-level elements of their cultures. Donald Trump, Boris Johnson and Scott Morrison are, in various ways, very different men. Also, none of them is held together by anything: each is a hologram. Trump is an American as everyone else imagines Americans; Johnson is the same for Britain, or at least England; as Morrison is for Australia.

This is a new development in our politics. Morrison's idol, John Howard, pretended to be ordinary, and understood how many Australians thought; but he was very far from ordinary himself, with sharp ideological beliefs and a vigorous mind. Bob Hawke was as smart as Howard, maybe smarter, and also classically Australian, in a certain way; but he was not what Australia was, but what Australians wished to be. Morrison, unlike his predecessors, is the symbolic perfection of a certain version of Australia.

Once, talking about racial division, he said, 'I know that Australia, as an idea – as an ideology even – and as an experience, will overwhelm these divisions.' Australia *as an ideology*. This is the most extreme expression of contentment and complacency imaginable. So satisfied is Morrison with Australia as it is that he believes it constitutes its own belief system. If you believe in Australia right now, in its current state, then that will overwhelm all else. This is not a country that is becoming, but a country that has arrived at its state of perfection. It is the promised land.

Isn't this how many Australians feel? We have beaches; we have good weather; we have abundant resources. We have grown rich on luck. But we do not feel uneasy with this luck, because we consider ourselves survivors, heroes in the battle against adversity – we deserve everything that we have. If Morrison is a man with no imagination, no real interest in either past or future, no ability to see outside himself, or to imagine that the world will not be what he wants it to be – an optimist, with optimism born of a life that has worked for him – then this, too, is the story of a large part of Australia.

There is a danger here, of mindlessly repeating Morrison's mistake, of falling into his marketing trap, of assuming that the quiet Australians, as he presents them, are Australia itself, and that he is exactly what he holds himself out to be, a perfect image of Australia as it really is. This would be to do his work for him, ignoring those parts of Australia for which he has so little feeling – the unquiet Australians. There are plenty of people who are not as Morrison presents them: who are not complacent, who understand that politics is not a game because they know with certainty its power over their lives.

But it would be as great a mistake to conclude that Morrison's success has little to tell us about ourselves. Faced with the accusation that 'Morrison is Australia', it is far too easy to say, 'Well, not me – I am completely different.' This would be yet another version of the same Australian trick: turning away from the aspects of ourselves we find the most unsettling and pretending they don't exist.

———

I speak from experience.

One night, about halfway through the writing of this book, I had a drink with a writer who told me that he dreams about the subjects of his biographical works. He asked me if I did the same. I told him no, and wondered, afterwards, if this was a poor reflection on my book – an indication that I had not sufficiently immersed myself in Scott Morrison's world.

Then, a month or two later, I had a strange dream – in fact, a strange set of dreams. I dreamed of Kevin Rudd, for whom I had worked. I dreamed, too, of Julia Gillard, for whom I had also worked. Finally, that night, I dreamed of Morrison.

Some dreams are difficult to decipher; their meaning is opaque, and therefore open to as many readings as there are interpreters. This was not one of those. In this dream, I interacted with Morrison, but the more notable fact was that, after a little while, people began mistaking me for him. People would come up to me on the street and ask to have their picture taken with me; I would have to remove my baseball cap to show them that I was not, in fact, Scott Morrison. At one point in the dream, I looked at myself in the mirror and I could see why this kept happening: the resemblance was uncanny.

This is not an unusual realisation for a writer to have. Janet Malcolm once asserted that a writer knows her subject intimately, 'because you have put a great deal of yourself into him … The characters of nonfiction, no less than those of fiction, derive from the writer's most idiosyncratic desires and deepest anxieties; they are what the writer wishes he was and worries that he is.'

If this is true of all writers and their subjects, it is perhaps particularly true in my case. I have never been a politician, but I have worked in two prime ministers' offices. There, I was a press secretary, or 'spin doctor'. My job was to construct stories that might be accepted by the media and by the public; to defend against the media's attempts to establish unhelpful facts; to present a crisp image rather than a set of complicated truths.

I was not as skilled at this as Morrison. Some of this was having less experience; some may have been less natural talent; and perhaps, I like to tell myself, I had more fidelity to truth, a greater loyalty to the world as it was.

In this book, I have, at times, taken a tone filled with distance and aloofness, the better to pass judgement on a man, a government, a political environment and a nation. I have used the term 'we' at times, to indicate that I am implicated, but this hardly overcomes the greater sense of separation from the elements that I have tried to judge with honesty and accuracy.

This is just another iteration of that great Australian habit, and perhaps that greater human habit, of splitting ourselves in two and casting off one half. Many of the criticisms I make in this book could be directed at me too. To varying degrees, this is true of most of us. We are happy to judge the government, even the nation, but are reluctant to judge our own role in events.

Soon, there will be an election. If Morrison wins, we will not say that it was because we embraced complacency or the reassuring triviality of treating politics as a game; it will be because we all succeeded together, in a time of crisis, through our own hard work, because that is what Australians do. If he loses, we will likely tell ourselves that his failures as prime minister were his own, and that they have nothing at all to say about the rest of us.

Acknowledgements

Many people made this book possible.

Chris Feik put the idea in my mind. Even more importantly, he was open to the type of book I wanted to write. Through the time it has taken, he has remained attentive, encouraging, firm and – at least so far as I can tell – honest with me. This book would not have been begun without his will; it would not have been finished without his brilliance and dedication.

I am as thankful to all those at Black Inc who have worked on the book. Kirstie Innes-Will, in particular, deserves immense thanks for her focus, speed, intelligence, diligence and keen eye. Julian Welch gave precise and insightful assistance. I am very glad, and very lucky, to have had Sallie Butler's devotion, energy and acuity in service of this book.

Morry Schwartz has been a champion of mine, and I could not be more grateful.

Several people very generously agreed to read drafts of this book. Each gave me important ideas and noticed gaps that would otherwise have gone unaddressed. Thank you to Helen Bauer, Judith Brett, Erik Jensen, Susan Knox, Robert Manne and Martin McKenzie-Murray.

My agent, Grace Heifetz, has provided constant support, encouragement and wisdom – thank you.

I am extremely fortunate to work with a number of superb editors who sharpen my writing and have, in various ways, helped me sharpen various ideas. At *The Sydney Morning Herald* and *The Age*, Julie Lewis deserves thanks, as do all of the editors who work with her: Rick Feneley, Catherine Naylor, Emily Day and Billy Cantwell. I am also grateful to James Chessell and Julie for putting their faith in me. Nick Feik at *The Monthly* commissioned a long piece on Scott Morrison from me in 2018. That was really the start of this book, and I thank him for coming up with the concept, for the confidence he placed in me and the fine work he did in shaping that piece. Natalie Book was sharp and generous as always.

My greatest thanks goes to Anne-Louise Sarks. She has read this book countless times and has always known what was needed. She has done this while preparing to take on a large job of her own, and while caring for our son Arlo, who arrived while this book was being written. I am in her debt always.

Finally, thank you to the many reporters whose work I have drawn upon. This book points to some of the failings of that profession. I would not have taken the time to make those arguments if I did not believe that journalism itself was invaluable. That there were facts to include in this book is just one small indication of that value.

Sources

APPEARANCES

Annabel Crabb, 'Scott Morrison', *Kitchen Cabinet*, ABC TV, 28 October 2015.

Brigid Delaney, 'Annabel Crabb: "I don't make *Kitchen Cabinet* so you can love it"', *The Guardian*, 12 November 2015.

Amy McQuire, 'Junk food journalism: Why Annabel Crabb's *Kitchen Cabinet* is toxic', *New Matilda*, 29 October 2015.

Ben Pobjie, 'What's on TV Wednesday: *Kitchen Cabinet* is good but may not be good for you', *The Sydney Morning Herald*, 2 November 2015.

Shannon Molloy, '*Kitchen Cabinet* with Annabel Crabb proves politicians can be human', News.com.au, 28 October 2015.

Eliza Borrello, 'Scott Morrison's Christmas Island visit slammed as "publicity stunt" by locals', ABC (online), 9 March 2019.

'When Gary met equality', *The Canberra Times*, 19 February 2011.

Scott Morrison, Radio 2GB interview, Media release, 16 February 2011.

'Morrison and Abbott stay down: Hockey joins them', Grog's Gamut blog, 16 February 2011, http://grogsgamut.blogspot.com/2011/02/morrison-and-abbott-stay-down-hockey.html, accessed 12 October 2021.

Jane Cadzow, 'The Watchman', *The Sydney Morning Herald*, 3 November 2012.

Helen McCabe, 'Who is Scott Morrison? The Prime Minister shares a rare and candid look inside his personal life', *The Australian Women's Weekly*, 20 March 2020.

Niki Savva, 'Tony Abbott's fate rests on Canning by-election result', *The Australian*, 20 August 2015.

'Annabel Crabb drops in on Scott Morrison, when *Kitchen Cabinet* returns Wednesday', *ABC Media Room*, 28 October 2015.

Katharine Murphy, 'From headkicker to suburban Scott: Will Morrison's rapid rebranding work?', *The Guardian*, 10 November 2018.

Scott Morrison, 'On Their Side', Address to the Liberal Party of Australia Federal Council, Sydney, 24 June 2017.

Scott Morrison, Press conference with the Minister for Education, Canberra, ACT, 20 September 2018.

Josh Bornstein, 'The ABC is like a victim trapped in an abusive relationship – with the government', *The Guardian*, 28 December 2015.

BLAMELESS

Malcolm Turnbull, Press conference, Parliament House, Canberra, 24 August 2019.

Malcolm Turnbull, *A Bigger Picture*, Hardie Grant, Melbourne, 2020.

David Crowe, 'Christian. Conservative. Ordinary. Cunning too. Scott Morrison's plan to become PM', *The Sydney Morning Herald*, 17 August 2018.

Sharri Markson & Sheradyn Holderhead, 'Conservative Coalition MPs urging Peter Dutton to replace Malcolm Turnbull 'within weeks', *The Daily Telegraph*, 17 August 2018, https://www.dailytelegraph.com.au/news/nsw/conservative-coalition-mps-urging-peter-dutton-to-replace-malcolm-turnbull-within-weeks/news-story/68ea9ee855c6b840ec6557985e4d359e

Sharri Markson, 'Dutton considers Turnbull challenge as PM backflips on 26pc emissions target', *The Daily Telegraph*, 18 August 2018, https://www.dailytelegraph.com.au/news/nsw/mps-who-say-prime-minister-has-shown-no-improvement-continue-to-back-home-affairs-minister/news-story/17a5efad65f5a6517b529f83599d6471

Daniel Hurst, 'Scott Morrison 'misled' public about role in Liberal coup, says Tony Abbott', *The Guardian*, 22 September 2015,

https://www.theguardian.com/australia-news/2015/sep/22/
scott-morrison-misled-public-about-role-in-liberal-coup-says-
tony-abbott

Peter Hartcher, "He was in it right up to his neck': How Scott
Morrison deposed a prime minister', *The Sydney Morning Herald*,
26 March 2019, https://www.smh.com.au/politics/federal/he-was-
in-it-right-up-to-his-neck-how-scott-morrison-deposed-a-prime-
minister-20190312-p513jl.html

AUTHENTIC

'Transcript of new prime minister Scott Morrison's first press conference',
Australian Financial Review, 24 August 2018.

Kate Lyons, "'Mesmerising": Boris Johnson's bizarre model buses claim
raises eyebrows', *The Guardian*, 26 June 2019.

Associated Press, 'Next Australian prime minister well placed to heal
party', *Fox News*, 23 August 2018.

Rachel Baxendale, 'Alan Tudge says the new PM has "authenticity" and
"instinct"', *The Australian*, 24 September 2018.

'Newspoll: Scott Morrison takes fight to Bill Shorten as preferred PM',
The Daily Telegraph, 15 October 2018.

House of Representatives, *Hansard*, 11 September 2018.

Michelle Grattan, 'Australians are increasingly non-partisan:
Morrison', *The Conversation*, 25 June 2017.

AAP, 'We need to connect with voters, Morrison', *The West Australian*,
24 June 2017.

'It's *The Muppet Show*: Scott Morrison says curtain has come down &
another gone up', Interview on *Sunrise*, 5 September 2018.

AAP, 'Curtains down on Muppet Show: PM Morrison', SBS (online),
5 September 2018.

AAP, 'PM: Cancel of COAG means less Tim Tams consumed in
Canberra', *The Herald Sun*, 20 September 2018.

Scott Morrison, Interview with Alan Jones, 2GB, 8 October 2018.

Sharri Markson, 'Curry-loving treasurer's new Budget has given him
hot new image', *The Daily Telegraph*, 24 June 2017.

Mark Ludlow, 'Scott Morrison: Faith, family and his beloved Cronulla Sharks', *Australian Financial Review*, 24 August 2018.

Scott Morrison, Twitter, 11 September 2009, https://mobile.twitter.com/scottmorrisonmp/status/3908921820, accessed 29 September 2021.

Andrew Tillettt, 'Morrison "not a phony" on the footy', *Australian Financial Review*, 15 April 2019.

Max Koslowski, '"He's got the personality to keep the party together": Howard backs Morrison to win the election', *The Sydney Morning Herald*, 4 December 2018.

House of Representatives, *Hansard*, 11 September 2018.

Sam Clench, 'Politics live: Scott Morrison faces second day in parliament', News.com.au, 11 September 2018.

Scott Morrison, Twitter, 18 September 2018, https://twitter.com/ScottMorrisonMP/status/24840509353, accessed 29 September 2021.

Samantha Maiden, 'Minister, who do you support? PM in hot water over footy colours', *The New Daily*, 15 April 2019.

PRAGMATIC

One Nation, 'Strawberry and diary industries facing hardship', Onenation.org, 20 September 2018.

Justin Sungil Park, 'Strawberry crisis: PM to raise jail sentence for food tampering to 15 years', SBS (online), 20 September 2018.

Michelle Grattan, 'Grattan on Friday: Morrison aims to make agility his prime ministerial trademark', *The Conversation*, 20 September 2018.

AAP Newswire, 'Morrison doing a lot but not on big issues', *Riverine Herald*, 20 September 2018.

Dennis Shanahan, 'Morrison's changes of pace take game to Labor', *The Australian*, 21 September 2018.

Graham Richardson, 'Bishop, Gichuhi, Sudmalis et al.: Spare me the bullying tales', *The Australian*, 21 September 2018.

Dennis Shanahan, 'With Turnbull gone, it's no longer a walkover for Shorten', *The Australian*, 22 September 2018.

David Speers, '"Action man Morrison not shy of policy reversal", *The Daily Telegraph*, 22 September 2018.

Michael Gordon, '"I'm not saying no to Gary": Treasurer reveals personal struggle behind NDIS budget decision', *The Sydney Morning Herald*, 10 March 2017.

Louise Yaxley, 'Dropping the Medicare levy hike is an awkward look for Scott Morrison after 2017's budget sell', ABC (online), 26 April 2018.

Scott Morrison, Speech, House of Representatives, *Hansard*, 14 February 2008.

Julia Baird with Scott Morrison, Shadow Immigration Minister, ABC Radio National, 21 August 2011.

Jane Cadzow, 'The Watchman', *The Sydney Morning Herald*, 3 November 2012.

Janet Malcolm interviewed by Katie Roiphe, 'Janet Malcolm, The Art of Nonfiction No. 4', *The Paris Review*, Spring 2011.

'I'm fresh for the fight of my life', News Limited, 26 August 2018.

Scott Morrison, Press conference – Operation Sovereign Borders Update, Australian Border Force, 8 November 2013.

Sean Kelly, 'Looking for Scott Morrison', *The Monthly*, November 2018.

Sarah Hanson-Young to Scott Morrison, Correspondence, 26 September 2014.

Michelle Grattan, 'Grattan on Friday: Morrison aims to make agility his prime ministerial trademark', *The Conversation*, 20 September 2018.

SUBURBAN

Donald Horne, *The Lucky Country*, Penguin Books, Sydney, 1964.

Donald Horne, *The Lucky Country*, 5th edn, Penguin Books, Sydney, 1998.

Eliza Barr, 'Prime Minister Scott Morrison to move to Kirribilli House', *The Daily Telegraph*, 25 September 2018.

Sharri Markson, 'Family guy: Scott Morrison on the core beliefs that drive him as PM', *The Daily Telegraph*, 21 September 2018.

Matthew Cranston, 'Scott Morrison is a property person's prime minister', *Australian Financial Review*, 27 August 2018.

Bevan Hurley, 'ScoMo Dundee: A future Aussie PM's role in New Zealand's great tourism wars', *Stuff*, 16 February 2020.

TourismAustraliaUSA, 'So Where the Bloody Hell are you?', YouTube, https://youtu.be/Y-ZLr9ePuj8, accessed 1 October 2021.

Annabel Crabb and Phillip Hudson, 'More "bloody" mess as tourism chief quits post', *The Age*, 12 March 2006.

'Tourism Australia seeks ideas to plug Oz', *The Sydney Morning Herald*, 19 June 2006.

'A big bloody controversy', *Marketing* magazine website, 9 June 2016, https://www.marketingmag.com.au/hubs-c/big-bloody- controversy/

SLEEPING SOUNDLY

Scott Morrison interview with Karl Stefanovic, *The Today Show*, 20 September 2018.

Ellien Whinnett, 'Immigration Minister Scott Morrison not immune to his job's hardline stance on asylum seekers', *Herald Sun*, 14 March 2014.

David Marr, 'Correspondence' on *The End of Certainty: Scott Morrison and Pandemic Politics*, in Laura Tingle, *The High Road: What Australia Can Learn from New Zealand*, Quarterly Essay 80, November 2020.

Katharine Murphy, *The End of Certainty: Scott Morrison and Pandemic Politics*, Quarterly Essay 79, September 2020.

Jane Cadzow, 'The Watchman', *The Sydney Morning Herald*, 3 November 2012.

James Wood, *How Fiction Works*, Farrar, Straus and Giroux, New York, 2008.

James Wood, 'Kazuo Ishiguro uses artificial intelligence to reveal the limits of our own', *The New Yorker*, 1 March 2021.

Tony Abbott, Interview with David Koch and Samantha Armytage, *Sunrise*, Seven Network, 10 September 2013.

E.M. Forster, *Aspects of the Novel*, Edward Arnold, UK, 1927.

TOGETHER

Scott Morrison, Twitter, 21 September 2018, https://twitter.com/dailytelegraph/status/1042992829742473216, accessed 29 September 2021.

Jasmine Burke, 'NSW council will move its Australia Day date',
    The Daily Telegraph, 21 September 2018.
Scott Morrison, 'Scott Morrison on Australia Day: Embrace national
    story on day it started', *The Courier Mail*, 25 September 2018.
Scott Morrison, Interview with Samantha Armytage and Natalie Barr,
    Sunrise, 25 September 2018.
John Howard, 1996 Sir Robert Menzies Lecture, 'The Liberal
    Tradition: The Beliefs and Values which Guide the Federal
    Government', 19 November 1996.
Scott Morrison, Doorstop interview, 25 September 2018.
Scott Morrison, Interview with Fran Kelly, ABC Radio National,
    26 September 2018.
Uluru Statement from the Heart, https://ulurustatement.org/the-
    statement
Richard Ferguson, 'Strewth: Marise sods off', *The Australian*,
    24 September 2018.

PROUD

Eliza Barr, 'Australia Day 2019 at Cronulla Beach: Photos', *The Daily
    Telegraph*, 26 January 2019, 26 January 2019.
Scott Morrison, Remarks, Western Sydney Airport, 24 September 2018.
Scott Morrison, Doorstop interview: Queenstown, Tasmania,
    5 October 2018.
ABC Politics, Twitter, 5 September 2018, https://twitter.com/politicsabc/
    status/1037158987118956544, accessed 29 September 2021.
Scott Morrison, Interview with Ben Fordham, 2GB,
    13 December 2018.
Scott Morrison, Addressing Task Group, Taji, Iraq, 20 December 2018.
Scott Morrison, Speech, 'A Stronger Economy; It's About People',
    29 January 2019.
Scott Morrison, Remarks, International Women's Day Parliamentary
    Breakfast, 14 February 2019.
Scott Morrison, Doorstop with Premier of South Australia, Minister
    for Defence, 14 October 2018.

Scott Morrison, Remarks, Albert Park, Fiji, 18 January 2018.

Scott Morrison, Speech, Minerals Council of Australia Dinner, 13 February 2019.

Scott Morrison, Remarks, Middle East Headquarters Region, 20 December 2018.

Scott Morrison, 'Listening to our quiet Australians', Opinion, 14 January 2019.

Scott Morrison, Interview with Paul Kennedy, *ABC News Breakfast*, ABC TV, 14 January 2019.

John Howard, Sir Robert Menzies Lecture, 19 November 1996.

Scott Morrison, Doorstop with the Minister for Cities, Urban Infrastructure & Population, 25 September 2018.

Scott Morrison, Doorstop, Canberra, ACT, 26 January 2019.

Scott Morrison, Speech, National Flag Raising and Citizenship Ceremony, 26 January 2019.

Scott Morrison, Address, Anzac Day Commemorative Service, 25 April 2020.

Ann Curthoys, 'The volatility of racism in Australia' in *Hate Speech and Freedom of Speech in Australia*, Vol. 2118, edited by Katharine Gelber and Adrienne Sarah Ackary Stone, Federation Press, 2007.

SECURE

'"Shorten can't be trusted on borders": Morrison's fury after losing asylum Medivac vote', *SBS News*, 12 February 2019.

Scott Morrison, Transcript, Jones & Co, 5 February 2019.

Ben Doherty, 'Delay to treatment of Hamid Kehazaei before he died revealed in leaked files', *The Guardian*, 28 November 2016.

Mark Willacy, Mark Solomons and Alex McDonald, 'Hamid Kehazaei case: Seriously ill asylum seeker forced to wait more than 24 hours for medical transfer', ABC (online), 8 December 2014.

Coroners Court, Brisbane, Findings of Inquest into the death of Hamid Khazei, 30 July 2018.

Ben Doherty, '"Begging to die": Succession of critically ill children moved off Nauru', *The Guardian*, 25 August 2018.

Erin Pearson, John Silvester and Simone Fox Koob, 'Lone terrorist responsible for deadly attack on Bourke Street', *The Age*, 9 November 2018.

Helen Davidson, 'Trolley man: Passers-by use chair and trolley to try to take down Melbourne attacker', *The Guardian*, 9 November 2018.

Scott Morrison, Press conference, Canberra, 13 February 2019.

Michael Koziol and David Wroe, 'Is this Scott Morrison's Tampa moment?', *The Sydney Morning Herald*, 12 February 2019.

Scott Morrison, Doorstop, Skye, Victoria, 6 February 2019.

Scott Morrison, Press Conference, Sydney, NSW, 10 November 2018.

Scott Morrison, National Press Club Address, 'Our Plan for Keeping Australians Safe and Secure', 11 February 2019.

Scott Morrison, Prime Minister's statement on the shooting incident in Christchurch, New Zealand, 15 March 2019.

Sean Kelly, 'Our PM is telling fairytales while Ardern does something radical', *The Sydney Morning Herald*, 16 March 2019.

Karl Ove Knausgård, 'The Inexplicable', *The New Yorker*, 25 May 2015.

Jeff Sparrow, 'Australia must reckon with the fact the Christchurch terrorist developed much of his hatred here', *The Guardian*, 10 December 2020.

Royal Commission of Inquiry into the Terrorist Attack on Christchurch Mosques on 15 March 2019, '2. The Terrorist Attack', https://christchurchattack.royalcommission.nz/the- report/part-1-purpose-and-process/the-terrorist-attack/

Jason Wilson, 'Do the Christchurch shootings expose the murderous nature of "ironic" online fascism?', *The Guardian*, 16 March 2019.

Parliament of Australia, Legal and Constitutional Affairs Legislation Committee, Migration Amendment (Repairing Medical Transfers) Bill 2019, 26 August 2019.

Miranda Devine, 'Prime Minister Scott Morrison recasts asylum seeker issue as electoral battleground', *The Daily Telegraph*, 12 February 2019.

Joe Hildebrand, 'Joe Hildebrand: The politics of people smuggling', News.com.au, 17 February 2019.

Caroline Overington, 'Scott Morrison banks on boats as Labor tries to shift conversation', *The Australian*, 13 February 2019.

RELAXED

Waleed Aly, *The Project*, Network Ten, 16 March 2019.

'Morrison dismisses anti-Muslim report as gossip', ABC News (online), 17 February 2011.

Scott Morrison, Interview with Waleed Aly, *The Project*, Network Ten, 21 March 2019.

Lenore Taylor, 'Morrison sees votes in anti-Muslim strategy', *The Sydney Morning Herald*, 17 February 2011.

Hannah Paine, '*Project* fights PM's "ugly" claims about Waleed Aly', News.com.au, 21 March 2019.

Scott Morrison on *News Breakfast*, ABC TV, 20 March 2019.

Laura Tingle, 'Coalition disarray spills into the open', *Australian Financial Review*, 19 February 2011.

'"PM doesn't hate Muslims": Community leader defends "friend" Scott Morrison', SBS Arabic24, 26 March 2013.

'Front page – Jones and Cronulla', *Media Watch*, ABC TV, 20 February 2006.

Emma Alberici, 'Alan Jones and 2GB breached Code of Practice: ACMA', *The World Today*, ABC TV, 10 April 2007.

'Defining Moments: Cronulla race riots', National Museum of Australia, www.nma.gov.au/defining-moments/resources/cronulla-race-riots, accessed 21 September 2021.

Scott Morrison, interviewed by Julia Baird, ABC Radio National, 21 August 2011.

Nick Bryant, 'The Shire versus Australia', *The Monthly*, June 2012.
'Blue ribbons, red rags', *The Australian*, 23 June 2007.

Simon Benson, 'Knives out in Liberal Party', *The Daily Telegraph*, 30 June 2007.

Andrew Clennell, Phillip Coorey and Kate McClymont, 'Now PM wants Towke dumped', *The Sydney Morning Herald*, 21 July 2007.

'NSW Libs to take no action against former candidate', ABC (online),
    16 August 2007.

Simon Benson, 'Ex-tourism boss still standing', *The Daily Telegraph*,
    25 August 2007.

Murray Trembat, 'Morrison confident: "I am up for any challenge"',
    St George and Sutherland Shire Leader, 13 March 2014.

J.M. Coetzee, 'Australia's Shame', *The New York Review of Books*,
    26 September 2019.

Peter Hartcher, 'Morrison's hammer v. Shorten's Allen key', *The Sydney
    Morning Herald*, 13 April 2019.

'Morrison promise: "You vote for me, you'll get me"', *7News*, Seven
    Network, 11 April 2019.

'Scott Morrison gives his final *7.30* interview of the 2019 campaign',
    7.30, ABC TV, 12 April 2019.

Peter Lewis, 'It's the unknown unknowns that will decide who wins the
    election', *The Guardian*, 16 May 2019.

Samantha Maiden, 'PM cancels interview, slaps down "lie" on alleged
    anti-Muslim chat', *The New Daily*, 20 March 2019.

Deborah Snow, 'Scott Morrison's relentless rise to power', *The Sydney
    Morning Herald*, 29 April 2016.

Amy Remeikis, 'Scott Morrison's Hawaii horror show: How a PR
    disaster unfolded', *The Guardian*, 21 December 2019.

VICTORY

Scott Morrison, Doorstop, United Nations, New York, 24 September
    2019.

Scott Morrison, Speech, Sydney, 18 May 2019.

Scott Morrison, Radio interview with Alan Jones, 2GB, 20 May 2019.

Sarah Martin, 'Scott Morrison warns Coalition MPs that election win
    did not give them a "blank cheque"', *The Guardian*, 23 July 2019.

Philip Coorey, 'Morrison sticks to "no change" election platform',
    Australian Financial Review, 20 May 2019.

'Scott Morrison brings a chunk of coal into parliament – video',
    The Guardian, 9 February 2019.

Scott Morrison, Facebook post, 14 December 2019, https://www. facebook.com/scottmorrison4cook/photos/date-night-with-jen-last-night-at-the-new-coliseum-theatre-in-western-sydney- gre/2856025281108523/, accessed 29 September 2021

Samantha Maiden, 'Scott Morrison escaped Sydney's bushfires on a business class flight to Hawaii', *The New Daily*, 18 December 2019.

Scott Morrison, Radio interview with John Stanley, 2GB, 20 December 2019.

Helen Davidson, '"We were surrounded": How the bushfires forced Rosedale families to flee to the beach', *The Guardian*, 2 January 2019.

'Scott Morrison heckled after he tries to shake hands with bushfire victim in NSW town of Cobargo', *The Guardian*, 2 January 2020.

Scott Morrison, Twitter, 4 January 2020, https://twitter.com/scottmorrisonmp/status/1213330419044638722, accessed 29 September 2021.

Joe McGinniss, *The Selling of the President 1968*, Trident Press, New York, 1969.

Joan Didion, 'Insider Baseball', *The New York Review of Books*, 27 October 1988.

FIRES

Greta Levy, '"Mate I think I'll take you down to Canberra": Scott Morrison suggests using Cronulla Sharks coach for a "rev up about how to play as one team" after chaotic Liberal leadership spill', *Daily Mail*, 8 September 2018.

Scott Morrison, Twitter, 20 November 2019, https://twitter.com/scottmorrisonmp/status/1197004347868999680?lang=en, accessed 29 September 2021

Scott Morrison, Remarks, New Year's Day, Cricket Australia, The Mcgrath Foundation Reception, 2 January 2020.

Liam Flanagan, Twitter, 1 January 2020, https://twitter.com/ljflannas/status/1212318131508527105?lang=en, accessed 29 September 2021.

Australian Associated Press, 'Hazard reduction burns are not a 'panacea' for bushfire risk, RFS boss says', *The Guardian*, 8 January 2020.

Naaman Zhou, 'Former Australian fire chiefs say Coalition ignored their advice because of climate change politics', *The Guardian*, 14 November 2019.

Scott Morrison, Press conference, Australian Parliament House, Canberra, ACT, 4 January 2020.

Scott Morrison, Press conference, Australian Parliament House, Canberra, ACT, 5 January 2020.

David Ross and Imogen Reid, 'Bushfires: Firebugs fuelling crisis as national arson toll hits 183', *The Australian*, 6 January 2020.

Scott Morrison, Doorstop interview, Kangaroo Island, 8 January 2020.

David Crowe, 'Deputy PM slams people raising climate change in relation to NSW bushfires', *The Sydney Morning Herald*, 11 November 2019.

Stephanie Dalzell, 'Adam Bandt defends "arsonists" comment by Greens colleague Jordon Steele-John', *Insiders*, ABC TV, 17 November 2019.

Scott Morrison, 'Scott Morrison's Hawaii horror show: How a PR disaster unfolded', *The Guardian*, 21 December 2019.

VIRUS

AAP, 'Prime Minister Scott Morrison calls for unity on Australia Day as he acknowledges a tough start to the year with bushfires, droughts and flooding', *The Daily Mail*, 26 January 2020.

Brett Worthington, 'Gatherings of more than 500 people to be cancelled, Australians urged not to travel overseas amid coronavirus fears', ABC (online), 14 March 2020.

Scott Morrison, Press conference, Australian Parliament House, Canberra, ACT, 8 May 2020.

Scott Morrison, Q&A, AFR Business Summit, Sydney, NSW, 10 March 2020.

Scott Morrison, 'Until the bell rings', Address to Menzies Research Centre, 6 September 2018.

Scott Morrison, Remarks, International Women's Day Women in
	Resources Breakfast, 8 March 2019.
Scott Morrison, Doorstop with Minister for Health and NSW Minister
	for Health, 23 September 2018.
Thomas J. Bollyky and Jennifer B. Nuzzo, 'Trump's "early" travel
	"bans", weren't bans and didn't work', *The Washington Post*,
	1 October 2020.

DIVISION

'Prime Minister Scott Morrison's speech to the Australian Christian
	Churches National Conference, Gold Coast – 2021', *Crikey*,
	28 April 2021.
Ally Foster, 'Jenny Morrison opens up about 14-year infertility
	struggle', News.com.au, 31 October 2019.
Sharri Markson, 'Family Guy: Scott Morrison on the core beliefs that
	drive him as PM', *The Daily Telegraph*, 21 September 2018.
Scott Morrison, Shadow Immigration Minister interview with Julia
	Baird, *ABC RN Sunday Profile*, 21 August 2011.
Jane Cadzow, 'The Watchman', *The Sydney Morning Herald*,
	3 November 2012.
Scott Morrison, 'Infertile couples paying a heavy price for Labor',
	Essential Baby, 28 March 2009.
Samantha Maiden, 'Scott Morrison talks faith, politics and creating
	Lara Bingle', *The Daily Telegraph*, 2 August 2013.
Helen Mccabe, 'Who is Scott Morrison? The Prime Minister shares
	a rare and candid look inside his personal life', *The Australian
	Women's Weekly*, 20 March 2020.
Scott Morrison, Speech, House of Representatives, *Hansard*,
	14 February 2008.
Miranda Wood and Linda Silmalis, 'Jenny Morrison opens up about
	her own battles and rallies support for mental health', *The Daily
	Telegraph*, 5 March 2019.
'"I still drive the kids to school": PM's wife Jenny Morrison gives first
	solo interview', 9Honey website, 16 February 2019.

Erik Jensen, *The Prosperity Gospel: How Scott Morrison won and Bill Shorten lost*, Quarterly Essay 74, 2019.

House of Representatives, *Hansard*, 22 July 2019.

House of Representatives, *Hansard*, 25 July 2019.

House of Representatives, *Hansard*, 1 August 2019.

Scott Morrison, Press conference, Australian Parliament House, Canberra, ACT, 20 March 2020.

Scott Morrison, Press conference, Australian Parliament House, Canberra, ACT, 16 July 2020.

Scott Morrison, Ministry meeting, 28 August 2018.

Scott Morrison, Interview on *Studio 10*, 27 May 2020.

James Boyce, 'The devil and Scott Morrison', *The Monthly*, February 2019.

VIOLENCE

Scott Morrison, Press conference, Australian Parliament House, Canberra, ACT, 23 March 2021.

Sarah Martin and Amanda Meade, 'Scott Morrison warns journalists to "be careful" with questions as he publicly airs media harassment claim', *The Guardian*, 23 March 2021.

Samantha Maiden, 'Young staffer Brittany Higgins says she was raped at Parliament House', News.com.au, 15 February 2021.

Scott Morrison, Doorstop interview, Australian Parliament House, Canberra, ACT, 16 February 2021.

Scott Morrison, Press conference, Kirribilli, NSW, 1 March 2021.

Sean Kelly, 'Hands-off Prime Minister prefers to share his humble pie', *The Sydney Morning Herald*, 23 August 2021.

Tom Lowrey and Jack Snape, 'Scott Morrison's "bullets" for protesters comment stuns Australian UN representative', ABC (online), 16 March 2021.

Samantha Maiden, 'Scott Morrison "not happy" Brittany Higgins' alleged rape was kept secret', News.com.au, 16 February 2021.

Scott Morrison, Interview with Ben Fordham, 2GB, 2 June 2020.

Scott Morrison, Interview with Ray Hadley, 2GB, 4 June 2020.

Scott Morrison, Press conference, Australian Parliament House, Canberra, ACT, 5 June 2020.

Jacqueline Rose, *On Violence and On Violence Against Women*, Faber & Faber, London, 2021

'Prime Minister Scott Morrison's speech to the Australian Christian Churches National Conference, Gold Coast – 2021', *Crikey*, 28 April 2021.

Scott Morrison, Doorstop, Parkville, Vic., 26 March 2021.

Scott Morrison, Remarks, International Women's Day, 8 March 2021.

Bernard Keane, 'Scott Morrison's incoherent speech reveals the confused nature of his core ideology', *Crikey*, 28 April 2021.

Jacqueline Maley, 'Inside our Pentecostal PM's church', *The Sydney Morning Herald*, 20 April 2019.

Helen Mccabe, 'Who is Scott Morrison? The Prime Minister shares a rare and candid look inside his personal life', *The Australian Women's Weekly*, 20 March 2020.

Judith Brett, 'Howard's heir: On Scott Morrison and his suburban aspirations', *The Monthly*, September 2019.

Katharine Murphy, *The End of Certainty: Scott Morrison And Pandemic Politics*, Quarterly Essay 79, September 2020.

James Boyce, 'The devil and Scott Morrison', *The Monthly*, February 2019.

T.M. Luhrmann, *How God Becomes Real: Kindling the Presence of Invisible Others*, Princeton University Press, 2020.

T.M. Luhrmann, *When God Talks Back: Understanding the American Evangelical Relationship with God*, Knopf Doubleday, New York, 2012.

Latika Bourke and Katina Curtis, "Distractions posing as solutions': Grace Tame criticises Scott Morrison's cabinet reshuffle', *The Sydney Morning Herald*, 31 March 2021.

Scott Morrison, Press conference, Raytheon Australia, Adelaide, SA, 31 March 2021.

PAST, PRESENT, FUTURE

Michelle Grattan, 'Grattan on Friday: COVID boxes Morrison in while Albanese hits the road', *The Conversation*, 15 July 2021.

Bree Gashparac, 'Jase demands apology from PM Scott Morrison after "nightmare" vaccine rollout', Kiis1011, 20 July 2021.

Scott Morrison, Press conference, Canberra, ACT, 22 July 2021.

Scott Morrison, Press conference, Australian Parliament House, Canberra, ACT, 14 August 2020.

Amber Schultz, 'The national cabinet's rules, processes and information are shrouded in secrecy', *Crikey*, 21 April 2020.

Prime Minister, Minister for Health, Minister for Industry, Science and Technology, 'New deal secures potential COVID-19 vaccine for every Australian', Media release, 19 August 2020.

Prime Minister, Minister for Health, 'Australia Secures a further 50 Million Doses of COVID-19 Vaccine', Media release, 5 November 2020.

Scott Morrison, Interview with *Today Show*, 11 March 2021.

Scott Morrison, Interview with *Sunrise*, 11 March 2021.

Scott Morrison, Doorstop, Castle Hill, NSW, 14 March 2021.

Scott Morrison, Press conference, Raytheon Australia, Adelaide, SA, 31 March 2021.

Scott Morrison, Interview with David Penberthy and Will Goodings, FiveAA, 21 July 2021.

Scott Morrison, Press conference, Canberra, ACT, 28 July 2021.

Farrah Tomazin and Clay Lucas, 'How did Australia's vaccine rollout turn into a "train wreck"?', *The Sydney Morning Herald*, 31 July 2021.

Janet Malcolm, *The Journalist and the Murderer*, Granta Books, London, 2011

Parliamentary debates, House of Representatives, *Hansard*, 2 October 2014.

EPILOGUE: MORRISON'S AUSTRALIA

These ideas about the excision of Christmas Island came to me
around the time I was reading *No Document* by Anwen Crawford
(Giramondo, 2021), which deals in part with Christmas Island;
I feel indebted to it.

SEAN KELLY is a columnist for *The Sydney Morning Herald* and *The Age* and a regular contributor to *The Monthly*. He was a political adviser to Julia Gillard and Kevin Rudd.